FISCHER vs.

SVETOZAR GLIGORIC

FISCHER

vs.

SPASSKY

*World Chess
Championship Match
1972*

Simon and Schuster
New York

SBN 671-21397-0 Casebound edition
SBN 671-21398-9 Fireside paperback edition
Library of Congress Catalog Card Number: 72-83892

Manufactured in the United States of America

CONTENTS

EXPLANATION OF SYMBOLS

+   check

0-0   castles king side

0-0-0   castles queen side

!   a strong move (sometimes used by Gligoric early in the game to show an important choice of opening move)

!!   a very strong move, usually winning very quickly

?   a bad move

??   a blunder, usually losing immediately

!?   a surprising or interesting move

?!   a doubtful move

INTRODUCTION

A scene shot by a Yugoslav film director at Bled in 1959 will remain an impressive momento of the world's chess in the latter half of the twentieth century. Tal raised his big, black eyes, looked at Fischer, and directed an overtly scornful smile at the sixteen-year-old boy. The manner in which he stared at his rival (rules of good manners ask for concentration upon the board) could only be accounted for by Tal's taking particular pleasure in psychologically challenging and outwitting his even younger rival who, absorbed in the problems of the play, was obviously unaware of what was going on around him.

At the closing banquet of that event (the Candidates' Tournament) Fischer complained to the author of this text of having lost four superior positions against Tal. Fischer's complaint was in vain. Tal had triumphed at the tournament and shortly afterwards he triumphed again in his first match with Botvinnik, thus marking his short but impressive reign as World Champion. This was probably the time when Fischer's indignation with Soviet chess players and their self-claimed superiority began.

When only a boy Fischer felt that his mission was to become the strongest player in the world Later he declared: 'Too many times, people don't try their best. They don't·have the keen spirit; the winning spirit. And once you make it you've got to guard your reputation — every day go in like an unknown to prove yourself. That's why I don't clown around. I don't believe in wasting time. My goal is to win the World Chess Championship; to beat the Russians (this is how Fischer always refers to the Soviet grandmasters although, for instance, Petrosian is Armenian and Keres Estonian). I take this very seriously.'

This is true. Fischer took the task more seriously than anybody else in the history of chess. It was his sister, who later married and moved to California, who initiated him in the rules of the game. Since the age of six he has thought only of chess. Later he quit school, then left his mother's flat in Brooklyn, and later still moved out of his home in Los Angeles and turned into a wanderer living in hotels and leaving his belongings behind. But not his wooden travelling chess set. 'Look at these pieces, smooth and light. No hard edges. Beautifully carved. The best set for playing with that I've ever seen. Here, feel this knight!'

After finally qualifying to meet Spassky, Fischer said: 'Someone has to stop them . . .' (the Soviets) '. . . I've been chosen. I intend to teach them a little humility.' Being aware of exaggeration in his statements Fischer admits privately that he does not know the reason for saying such things occasionally, but 'Such moods do come now and then.' He has been following the Soviet press for years and what it has written about him. Why this involvement in opinions in a country thousands of miles away; opinions few others in America either know or care about?

'I'm sick of their hypocrisy . . .' says Fischer. '. . . like when I beat Petrosian. There was just a little squib in their papers about it. But there was a local championship that they put in headlines. If Petrosian had beaten me *then* there would have been headlines.'

Recognition (all the time) and fair play (since the Candidates' Tournament at Curacao in 1962) have not been the only subjects of Fischer's indignity with the Soviets. It has been money too. He believes that he has been systematically excluded from earning money, since the Soviet government pays its players and sends them to tournaments 'free' (i.e. without demanding an appearance fee) while he insists on extra fees thereby incurring unfavourable world opinion. 'They would send top Russian players globe-trotting to play free in places where I was asking thousands of dollars. Well, I've finally broken through this . . .' (their conspiracy against him) '. . . but for about a year and eight months in 1969 and 1970 I was pretty discouraged. I refused to play the Russians and they have most of the best players in the world. For a time I was thinking of quitting international chess. But then I thought 'What else can I do?'. The answer was 'Nothing'.'

Fischer is very angry because, he says, he has been the world's best chess player since he was 18 and has had little recognition of this. In particular, he has not become wealthy as befits a champion — as, in fact, befits the world's all-time greatest player (according to the rating system employed by F.I.D.E). Part of his dissatisfaction falls on America. 'I was even put down in my own country. Americans really don't know much about chess. So they listened to other people. But I think when I beat Spassky, that Americans will take a greater interest in chess. Americans like winners . . . . The U.S. is not a cultural country. The people here want to be entertained. They don't want any mental strain, and chess is a high intellectual form. Americans want to plunk in front of a TV and not to have to open a book . . . But now, President Nixon just sent me a letter saying that America is backing me.'

Thus, for Fischer, his match with Spassky is the match of his life against Soviet chess. There is not much reason for Fischer to be angry with Spassky personally. His opponent, six years older than he, has always treated him in a friendly and sympathetic way. (Spassky told me once privately, with some irony at his own expense, that it would suit him best if he moved around the world and, like a philosopher, studied human relationships.)

If he senses simple sincerity in others, Fischer becomes disarmed. This is why he seems (unconsciously) to dislike remembering, before the big match, the moments of friendship which he experienced with Spassky at Santa Monica in 1966 and elsewhere. That could only upset his psychological armament against his principal opponent.

But Fischer does have friends. Quinteros, a young master from Argentina exclaimed in Buenos Aires during the Fischer-Petrosian match: 'Pressmen have been doing Fischer wrong all his life. He loves chess immensely and he is a wonderful friend.' Fischer's openness to those who show their good intentions contrasts with his sulkiness to the whole world, and particularly to the Soviet chess circle.

I cannot but help remembering one particular detail. When I had an intercontinental interview with both of them for Radio Belgrade, Fischer started his conversation in an angry tone saying that Spassky had been making preparations to meet him for three years while he had only two months to prepare (which was the time that had elapsed since his match with Petrosian). However, when I told him that Spassky too wanted the match to begin as late as possible, he was unpleasantly surprised rather than glad. He had acquired the habit in his previous negotiations of following the rule, instinctively rather than by reason, 'all that the rival does not want has to be good for me'. But now he was at a loss what to demand when their wishes coincided. His first reaction was to try to avoid committing himself to any statement. Exhausting negotiations suited the edifice of truculence that the American had erected round his chess better than an easy coming to terms.

While Spassky himself, on my suggestion in a telephone conversation, was inclined to support the idea of going to F.I.D.E.'s H.Q. there to talk about the place and the time of the match. Bobby was less enthusiastic about the chance to meet his rival before the match. 'No friendship' seems to have been Fischer's concealed anxiety. However, in reality things took the opposite course. For fear that he might lose his best financial offer Fischer did come to Amsterdam (100,000 dollars a year was Fischer's personal plan during the first year of both the new era of his life and his different status in business-orientated American society). In Amsterdam it was Spassky who was the absent one. The World Champion wanted to press more strongly and to force his choice of venue for more favourable climatic and other conditions for himself. The Soviet side had their own reasons for not compromising. Fischer had played all his matches on the American side of the Atlantic. They had had enough of favouring the younger rival. The World Champion had his own rights and he would not go all the way to Fischer's back yard as the others had gone. Nor would he play in the south of Europe in summer heat to which he had not been accustomed. Now was the time for Fischer to concede.

From a list of seventeen offers, eight possible venues were selected for serious consideration. Then came the first surprising move. The Soviet order of preference was limited to four places: 1 Reykjavik, 2 Amsterdam, 3 Dortmund, 4 Paris. The other four offers were rejected through the Soviet embassy in the Netherlands which proclaimed that they were 'unacceptable to Spassky'. Now it was the turn of Fischer's manager Ed Edmondson (the Executive Director of the U.S.C.F.) to make the appropriate move. Fischer himself, while in Amsterdam, uttered only three words to Dutch journalists — I don't know' — when they asked him if he agreed to play in the Netherlands. A single repetition on the American list of any one place from the Soviet list would mean a free hand for F.I.D.E. President Dr Euwe to appoint that place as the venue as the 'only possible choice by agreement of the two rivals'. But such an agreement might have reduced by half Fischer's income from the match for which he had been working all his life. After several hour's reflection, Edmondson's decision in this diplomatic game of hide and seek was infallible: the cities of Southern Europe were certainly not on Spassky's list (that is two towns in Yugoslavia, 1 Belgrade, 2 Sarajevo); nor would the two transatlantic cities be on the Soviet list (3 Buenos Aires, 4 Montreal). Thus no city was on both lists. The first round of this particular match ended in a draw. Fischer actually liked Buenos Aires best but it had laid an insufficient guaranteed sum which prevented it from being promoted to first place on his list.

A new attempt at an agreement came when Edmondson visited Moscow but this did not bear fruit. Although Reykjavik was not a bad choice (125,000 dollars for the prize fund against 152,000 dollars offered by Belgrade) Fischer, in New York, followed his sacred rule not to accept on principle his rival's suggestions. And why? When it became clear that the disagreement resembled a Gordian knot Dr Euwe cut it in the manner of Alexander the Great and decided to divide the match into two halves: twelve games in Belgrade and the remainder, up to a maximum of twelve, in Reykjavik. This was not an ideal solution but it had its precedent when players of different countries were concerned — in 1948 Botvinnik won the title in the match-tournament which was played one half in the Netherlands and the other in the Soviet Union. And after all, what else could Dr Euwe do if he wanted to be impartial in the eyes of F.I.D.E. members? Outspokenness has become more fashionable than the so-called gentlemanly kindness. Neither Spassky nor Fischer showed any particular consideration for his rival's desires. Fischer did not try to conceal his aspiration to take his opponent across the ocean ('the Russians play worse there') nor Spassky his wish to play in the Far North because 'Iceland reminded me most of the climate in my native Leningrad'.

The Soviet Chess Federation made a sharp protest against Euwe's solution: 'Spassky cannot accept the Belgrade summer although we respect the conditions offered'. The American magazine *Time* said that the decision had been borrowed from King Solomon.

Fischer did not want to commend Euwe's decision either: 'It's a mistake. You will have double the problems. People are going to be confused, moving around, and it will seem like a road show. I don't like it!' In fact Bobby was not actually angry Reykjavik was only unacceptable to him for tactical reasons and he was the first of the two to concede to the division of the match. His statement to F.I.D.E.: 'Prefer all games Belgrade starting June 25 but will abide by your decision start between June 21 and 25 split between first Belgrade then Reykjavik.'. His statement for the American public: 'It's going to be over in a couple of months and then I'll be Champion!'

For Spassky, concession was a more difficult process. It seemed again, at least to a slight degree, that Fischer's demands had been met more fully than his own. The reason lay partially in the fact that the starting points of the Soviet side were less elastic. But at any rate, Dr Euwe's decision did not stand for long. At the beginning of April 'the biggest match' was unexpectedly put in question. Fischer, who admits himself that he is 'unpredictable', all of a sudden didn't want to play under the conditions of the agreement reached on his behalf, as well as Spassky's, in Amsterdam. Under the wrong impression that his interests were neglected by F.I.D.E. and the organisers, and that the American federation was 'compromising too much in fear that the Soviet federation might cancel the match', Fischer refrained from employing any representative and took the whole thing into his own hands.

This meant that after protracted arguments and discussions, mostly carried out by intercontinental telephone calls and cables, the President of F.I.D.E. was forced to put an ultimatum to the challenger: He or Petrosian? For, in the face of new financial demands by Fischer, the Belgrade organizer cancelled his offer and the Sovet Federation energetically refused new bids for the venue, asking that Iceland's offer be respected in accordance with the previously reached agreement.

At the very last moment, when the chess world didn't know whether it would have a Spassky-Fischer match in Reykjavik or a Spassky-Petrosian match in Moscow, Fischer accepted the terms through his newly chosen lawyer. The biggest match had been saved . . .

But only in appearance. When Fischer was due to be in Iceland to start the match, he was instead in New York, repeating his claim for thirty per cent of the gate money for each of the players. This demand, for financal reasons, could not be accepted by the organizers.

Even Spassky, who had been in Reykjavik for about two weeks before the match was due to begin, believed that all possibility of the match taking place was over. Fischer was not present at the big opening ceremony on the night of Saturday July 1st, nor the next day when the first game should have been played. Probably Fischer, still in New York at the twenty-fifth hour, had the same pessimistic opinion as Spassky. Was he reasoning that 'Clay would never agree to be deprived of his percentage of the gate money'? (Why should chess champions be treated on a lower level than boxers?) Perhaps Fischer had instinctively lost the will to play Spassky at the moment when the title holder might still be in his prime and it was this that made him stay away. We shall never know.

In order to bring the Icelandic organisers out of their consternation (so much money had been spent on preparing for the match) and to save the interests of world chess, the President of F.I.D.E., Dr Euwe, took the risk of making the (perhaps judicially wrong) decision to delay the first game for two days. This unexpected decision gave Fischer a little more time in the hope that he would 'come to his senses'. This would not have helped much if, on the same day, the *deus ex machina* had not appeared in the person of British chess sponsor Jim Slater who simply added £50,000 to the Icelandic prize fund of 125,000 dollars. His message to Fischer was: 'If money is the question, here it is. Now come out and play, chicken!'

Robert Fischer landed on Icelandic tarmac early on the morning of Tuesday July 4th and before Dr Euwe's noon deadline. But the first game was delayed again because the champion did not agree to the drawing of lots until Fischer apologized for 'having violated the rules' by his late arrival.

The atmosphere was such that the majority placed Fischer as favourite for the forthcoming meeting. In an inquiry amongst the contestants and experts at Hastings in January, only one International Master said: 'I don't know what Fischer can play against

Spassky's queen's pawn. Fischer hasn't got a good defence.' Almost everyone else forecast that Fischer would win easily, and the most voluble was Najdorf who had witnessed Fischer's play against Petrosian at Buenos Aires.

Spassky's remarkable scores in matches and his chameleon-like ability to adapt himself to any rival had been forgotten. An exceptionally intelligent observer of people, Spassky is a very cunning and dangerous rival. Let us remember, for example, how he waited for Larsen to start playing heedlessly in their match in Malmo. In contrast, Fischer, against the same rival last year in Denver, went in a straight line trying to play better in general. Spassky defeated some by patience (Korchnoi, after losing the Candidates' final in 1968: 'Spassky has taught me not to push pawns too far.'); he defeated Geller with mating attacks, Tal by enterprising play without counting material (which is Tal's way of thinking), Petrosian (the most difficult) by a sudden rousing of energy in himself in the final stage of the match when Petrosian ceased to strive, believing he would win the fight. The end of that match must have looked to Petrosian like waking from a short, ugly dream.

All this has tended to be overlooked in the face of Fischer's most impressive results and Spassky's insufficiently ambitious play in recent events. (Donner: 'Spassky is stronger but I am afraid that he unconsciously wishes to lose the match.'.)

Fischer has said of Spassky's play in Gothenburg (August 1971): 'He has the title and is little interested in anything else.'. Fischer's intensity of creativity in games is always on the same level, while Spassky vacillates and behaves more casually in that respect. This is, perhaps, the reason why in the games of Fischer's matches there are fewer mistakes than in Spassky's.

To what degree had Spassky succeeded in arming himself psychologically for the match against his very ambitious challenger? The obligation to defend the recognised chess empire from assaults and destruction is a great responsibility and stimulus, but it could be a terrible burden also. However, when the fight begins he will defend himself. Before his second match with Petrosian he said privately: 'This time we'll fight without mercy. Even friendship may leave'.

Spassky can feel respect but he is not impressionable. Of Petrosian's play in the latter half of the match in Buenos Aires he said: '. . . like a child'! Speaking from the experience of his second match with Petrosian he says: '. . . the regulation which states that a score of 12-12 leaves the title with the champion is a handicap for the challenger. On the other hand this regulation leads the champion to play more cautious 'never lose' tactics. Such tactics are in practice risky against a rival who ventures something . . . Petrosian's tactics were too passive, too cautious. and this was the main reason for his defeat. I, for my part, shall draw the moral therefrom and will never use such tactics.'

Spassky has already prepared for Fischer once before, in anticipation of the match between the Soviet Union and the Rest of the World in Belgrade in 1970. He and Botvinnik concluded that Fischer's style was 'too simple' and that it was easy to see through Fischer's aim in the game. But speaking of the abortive unofficial match between Fischer and Botvinnik that was planned for the Netherlands, Spassky said: '. . . Botvinnik was an optimist. This is funny. For me it is very funny. I think this match would be very hard for Botvinnik.'

Taking a look at Spassky's twenty year career, the vast majority of his successes can be seen to have taken place at home, in terrible competition with the top Soviet grandmasters. This makes for a practical experience such as Fischer could never get. But, by way of compensation, Fischer seems to have exceeded Spassky and Soviet grandmasters in general in his highest professional attitude to chess. Answering a *Life* reporter about his way of preparing for the match, Fischer did not know what to say: 'I will be walking round as usual. I will be looking at chess . . .' In fact, whereas preparation means, for Spassky, an exceptional life style (this is why he preferred the match to begin later — a point which Fischer was unable to grasp immediately), for Fischer it brings about no change in his everyday life's routine. In this lies an important advantage — his 'player's engine is constantly chugging'.

It was quite natural for Fischer to be more optimistic in an interview on Radio Belgrade. When I asked him if the match would go to the maximum 24 games he replied in the negative, while Spassky is different and said that he would know the answer 'only when my preparations are finished in May'.

While walking with me once, Spassky, who was already World Champion at the time, confessed his wish to forget all that he knew, like a superfluous load, and to start thinking about chess from the beginning. What enormous creative ambition in a man who is called casual by some!

In practice, Fischer has more often manifested an impeccable treatment of various positions, especially in the opening. In fact, only one question remains open. Who actually knows more about chess — Spassky or Fischer?

The challenger was, perhaps, right when he claimed: 'It will probably be the greatest sports event in history. Bigger even than the Frazier-Ali fight . . .'

FISCHER'S PLAYING RECORD

Tournaments

		Place	W	D	L
1956	Rosenwald Trophy	8th	2	5	4
1957/8	USA Ch.	1st	8	5	0
1958	Portoroz Interzonal	5th-6th	6	12	2
1958/9	USA Ch.	1st	6	5	0
1959	Mar del Plata	3rd-4th	8	4	2
	Santiago	4th-7th	7	1	4
	Zurich	3rd-4th	8	5	2
	Candidates' Tournament (Yugoslavia)	5th-6th	8	9	11
1959/60	USA Ch.	1st	7	4	0
1960	Mar del Plata	1st-2nd	13	1	1
	Buenos Aires	13th	2	11	5
	Reykjavik	1st	3	1	0
	Olympiad (Leipzig)		10	6	2
1960/1	USA Ch.	1st	7	4	0
1961	Bled	2nd	8	11	0
1962	Stockholm Interzonal	1st	13	9	0
	Curacao Candidates' Tournament	4th	8	12	7
	Olympiad (Varna)		8	6	3
1962/3	USA Ch.	1st	6	4	1
1963/4	USA Ch.	1st	11	0	0
1965	Havana (by telex)	2nd-4th	12	6	3
1965/6	USA Ch.	1st	8	1	2
1966	Santa Monica	2nd	7	8	3
	Olympiad (Havana)		14	2	1
1966/7	USA Ch.	1st	8	3	0
1967	Monaco	1st	6	2	1
	Skopje	1st	12	3	2
	Sousse Interzonal withdrew while leading		7	3	0
1968	Netanya	1st	10	3	0
	Vinkovci	1st	9	4	0
1970	USSR v Rest of the World match (Board 2 v Petrosian)		2	2	0
	Rovinj/Zagreb	1st	10	6	1
	Buenos Aires	1st	13	4	0
	Olympiad (Siegen)		8	4	1
	Palma Interzonal	1st	15	7	1

Total 290 wins 173 draws 59 losses = 72%

Matches

Year	Opponent	Result			
1961	Reshevsky	unfinished	2	7	2
1971	Taimanov	won	6	0	0
	Larsen	won	6	0	0
	Petrosian	won	5	3	1

Total 19 wins 10 draws 3 losses = 75%

SPASSKY'S PLAYING RECORD

Tournaments

		Place	W	D	L
1952	Leningrad Ch.	2nd	6	7	0
1953	Bucharest	4th-5th	8	8	3
1954	Young Masters Tournament	1st	10	5	0
	Semi-final USSR Ch.	4th	6	12	2
1955	22nd USSR Ch.	3rd-4th	7	9	3
	World Junior Ch. (Antwerp)	1st	13	2	1
	Gothenburg Interzonal	8th-9th	7	8	5
	Student Olympiad (Lyons)		7	1	0
1956	23rd USSR Ch.	1st-3rd	7	9	1
	USSR Ch. play-off	3rd	0	1	3
	Amsterdam Candidates'	3rd-8th	3	13	2
	Semi-final USSR Ch.	1st-5th	7	9	3
1957	24th USSR Ch.	4th-5th	7	12	2
	Student Olympiad (Reykjavik)		5	4	0
	European Team Ch. (Hamburg)		2	3	0
	Semi-final USSR Ch.	1st-2nd	7	11	1
1958	25th USSR Ch.	5th-6th	7	7	4
	Student Olympiad (Varna)		4	5	0
	Semi-final USSR Ch.	1st-2nd	7	6	2
1959	26th USSR Ch.	2nd-3rd	8	9	2
	Moscow Central Chess Club Ch.	1st-3rd	4	6	1
	Leningrad Ch.	1st	11	6	0
	Semi-final USSR Ch.	1st-2nd	9	5	1
	Spartakiad		4	4	0
	Riga	1st	10	3	0
1960	27th USSR Ch.	9th-10th	5	10	4
	Mar del Plata	1st-2nd	12	3	0
	Student Olympiad (Leningrad)		0	2	1
	USSR Team Ch.		3	5	0
	Trud Trade Union Ch.	1st	8	7	0
	Semi-final USSR Ch.	1st	8	8	1
1961	28th USSR Ch.	5th-6th	7	8	4
	Leningrad Ch.	1st-2nd	8	10	0
	29th USSR Ch.	1st	10	9	1
1962	Student Olympiad (Marienbad)		6	3	0
	Havana	2nd-3rd	11	10	0
	Olympiad (Varna)		8	6	0
	USSR Team Ch.		4	4	0
	30th USSR Ch.	5th	9	7	3

1963	Semi-final USSR Ch.	2nd	6	9	0
	31st USSR Ch.	1st-3rd	5	14	0
1964	USSR Ch. play-off	2nd	1	2	1
	Zonal Tournament (Moscow)	1st	4	6	2
	Amsterdam Interzonal	1st-4th	13	8	2
	Sochi	4th	5	9	1
	Belgrade	1st	9	8	0
	Olympiad (Tel Aviv)		8	6	0
1965	Trades Union Spartakiad		3	4	0
	Sochi	1st-2nd	6	9	0
	Hastings	1st-2nd	6	3	0
1966	Santa Monica	1st	5	13	0
	USSR Team Ch.		0	9	1
	Sochi	5th-6th	6	7	1
	Olympiad (Havana)		5	10	0
1967	Beverwijk	1st	7	8	0
	RSFSR Ch.	1st-2nd	6	5	0
	Moscow	6th-8th	4	11	2
	Spartakiad		3	5	0
	Sochi	1st-5th	5	10	0
	Winnipeg	3rd-4th	2	7	0
1968	Olympiad (Lugano)		6	8	0
	Palma	2nd-3rd	10	6	1
1969	San Juan	1st	8	7	0
	Palma	5th	3	14	0
1970	USSR v Rest of the World match				
	(Board 1 v Larsen)		1	1	1
	Leiden	1st	2	10	0
	Amsterdam	1st-2nd	8	7	0
	Olympiad (Siegen)		7	5	0
1971	Gothenburg	3rd	5	6	0
	USSR Team Ch.		3	1	0
	Moscow	6th-7th	4	11	2

Total 431 wins 496 draws 64 losses = 68.5%

Matches

1965	Keres	won	4	4	2
	Geller	won	3	5	0
	Tal	won	4	5	1
1966	Petrosian	lost	3	17	4
1968	Geller	won	3	5	0
	Larsen	won	4	3	1
	Korchnoy	won	4	5	1
1969	Petrosian	won	6	13	4

Total 31 wins 57 draws 13 losses = 58.9%

PREVIOUS ENCOUNTERS

Although Fischer and Spassky are two of the young 'veterans' of the international tournament circuit, they had only met over the board five times before this match. It is these five games that added so much interest to the match, not because of the games themselves but because of their results.

The simple truth is that Fischer had never beaten Spassky! The American has a plus score against most international players, but he had not managed a single win against the Russian.

So, although most forecasters tipped Fischer to win in Reykjavik, most of them qualified their statements. The five reasons for these qualifications we give below, with light notes.

White: Spassky
Black: Fischer
Mar del Plata, 1960
King's Gambit

1	P—K4	P—K4
2	P—KB4	PxP
3	N—KB3	P—KN4

After this game Fischer wrote a famous article "The King's Gambit is busted" in which he recommended 3 ... P-Q3 as the correct defence.

4	P—KR4	P—N5
5	N—K5	N—KB3
6	P—Q4	P—Q3
7	N—Q3	NxP
8	BxP	B—N2

9 N—B3?
Better is 9 P-B3.

9	...	NxN
10	PxN	P—QB4
11	B—K2	PxP
12	0—0	N—B3
13	BxNP	0—0
14	BxB	RxB
15	Q—N4	P—B4

Fischer's suggestion 15 ... K-R1 is safer.

16	Q—N3	PxP
17	QR—K1!	K—R1

18 K—R1?
Fischer preferred the immediate capture 18 BxP. e.g. 18 ... R-KN1 19 N-K5!

18	...	R—KN1
19	BxP!	B—B1!
20	B—K5+	NxB
21	QxN+	R—N2!

Winning the KRP.

22   RxP

If 22 R-B4? B-Q3 or 22 P-R5 Q-N4.

22	...	QxP+
23	K—N1	

23   ...   Q—N5?

Correct is 23 ... Q-N6! 24 QxQ RxQ (threatening ... RxN followed by ... P-B7) and White is in a bad way.

24	R—B2	B—K2
25	R—K4	

25   ...   Q—N4?

Black can force a draw by repetition: 25 ... Q-Q8+ 26 R-K1 Q-N5 27 R-K4 Q-Q8+ etc. — Fischer.

26   Q—Q4!   R—KB1?

26 ... B-B1 is good enough for a draw. e.g. 27 QxRP B-B4 28 NxB QxN 29 R-K8+ R-N1, or 27 N-K5 B-B4! 28 N-B7+ K-N1.

27	R—K5!	R—Q1

Or 27 ... Q-N3 28 RxB winning.

28	Q—K4	Q—R5
29	R—B4	**Resigns**

White: Spassky
Black: Fischer
Second Piatigorsky Cup.
Santa Monica, 1966
Grunfeld Defence

1	P—Q4	N—KB3
2	P—QB4	P—KN3
3	N—QB3	P—Q4
4	PxP	NxP
5	P—K4	NxN
6	PxN	B—N2
7	B—QB4	P—QB4
8	N—K2	N—B3
9	B—K3	O—O
10	O—O	Q—B2
11	R—B1	R—Q1
12	Q—K1	P—K3

12 ... Q-R4! is stronger, and if 13 PxP or 13 P-Q5 then 13 ... N-K4! — Spassky.

13	P—B4	N—R4
14	B—Q3	P—B4
15	R—Q1	P—N3
16	Q—B2	PxQP
17	BxP	BxB

18	PxB	B—N2
19	N—N3	Q—B2
20	P—Q5!	

Opening up Fischer's king.

20	...	BPxP
21	PxP	QxKP
22	P—B5	Q—B2

Not 22 ... PxP 23 NxBP Q-KB3 because of 24 Q-K3 when White has a crushing attack.

| 23 | BxP | RxR |
| 24 | RxR | R—KB1! |

And not 24 ... BxB 25 NxB QxBP 26 N-B6+ K-N2 27 R-Q7+ KxN 28 Q-R4+ again with a winning attack.

25	B—N1	Q—B3
26	Q—B2	K—R1
27	PxP	PxP
28	Q—Q2	K—N2
29	R—KB1	Q—K2
30	Q—Q4+	R—B3
31	N—K4	BxN
32	BxB	Q—B4
33	QxQ	

| 33 | ... | RxR+? |

Spassky praised Fischer's conduct of the defence up to this point. But here he suggests 33 ... PxQ with good chances for a draw, e.g. 34 RxR KxR 35 P-KR4 N-B5 36 K-B2 N-Q3, or 34 R-B1 P-B5 35 R-B3 R-K3 36 B-B3 K-B3 37 K-B2 P-N4.

34	KxR	PxQ
35	P—KR4	N—B5
36	K—K2	N—K4
37	K—K3	K—B3
38	K—B4	N—B2

| 39 | K—K3 | |

39 B-Q5 would have been more accurate since now Black can play 39 ... N-Q3 when the win is difficult to force.

39	...	P—N4?
40	P—R5	N—R3
41	K—Q3	K—K4
42	B—R8	K—Q3
43	K—B4	P—N5
44	P—R4	N—N1
45	P—R5	N—R3

46	B—K4	P—N6
47	K—N5	N—N1
48	B—N1	N—R3
49	K—R6	K—B3
50	B—R2	Resigns

White: Fischer
Black: Spassky
Second Piatigorsky Cup.
Santa Monica, 1966
Ruy Lopez

1	P—K4	P—K4
2	N—KB3	N—QB3
3	B—N5	P—QR3
4	B—R4	N—B3
5	0—0	B—K2
6	R—K1	P—QN4
7	B—N3	0—0
8	P—B3	P—Q4

9	PxP	NxP
10	NxP	NxN
11	RxN	P—QB3
12	P—N3	N—B3
13	P—Q4	B—Q3
14	R—K1	B—KN5
15	Q—Q3	

15 P-B3 B-KB4 16 B-N5 P-B4 also gives
Black compensation for the pawn.

15	...	P—B4
16	PxP	BxBP
17	QxQ	QRxQ
18	B—KB4	P—R3
19	N—R3	P—N4
20	B—K3	

If 20 B-K5 R-Q7 and if then 21 BxN?
BxP+ winning.

20	...	BxB
21	RxB	R—Q7

22	N—B2	R—K1
23	RxR+	NxR
24	N—K3	B—B6
25	B—B2	N—Q3

26	P—N3	K—B1
27	P—QR4	N—K5
28	BxN	BxB
29	PxP	PxP
30	P—QN4	R—N7

31	P—N4	K—N2
32	K—B1	K—B3
33	R—R5	R—N8+
34	K—K2	R—N7+
35	K—B1	

Draw agreed.

White: Fischer
Black: Spassky
Havana Olympiad, 1966
Ruy Lopez

1	P—K4	P—K4
2	N—KB3	N—QB3
3	B—N5	P—QR3
4	B—R4	N—B3
5	0—0	B—K2
6	R—K1	P—QN4
7	B—N3	0—0
8	P—B3	P—Q3
9	P—KR3	P—R3
10	P—Q4	R—K1
11	QN—Q2	B—B1
12	N—B1	B—Q2

13	N—N3	N—QR4
14	B—B2	P—B4
15	P—N3	BPxP

Spassky prefers White's game after 15 ...
N-B3 16 P-Q5.

16	PxP	N—B3
17	B—N2	P—N3
18	Q—Q2	B—N2
19	QR—Q1	Q—N3
20	N—B1	QR—Q1
21	N—K3	Q—N1
22	B—N1	Q—N2
23	R—QB1	K—R2

If 23 ... PxP 24 NxP NxP 25 BxN RxB 26
NxN BxN 27 BxB KxB 28 Q-B3+ winning a
piece.

24	P—R3	B—QB1
25	B—B3	B—Q2
26	Q—N2	Q—N1
27	P—QN4!	K—N1
28	QR—Q1	N—KR2
29	B—R2	N—N4
30	NxN	PxN
31	PxP	PxP

After 31 ... NxKP, 32 N-Q5 is still strong.

32 N—Q5   N—K2

If 32 ... N-Q5 (which was suggested by many of the kibbitzers), 33 Q-Q2 N-K3 34 P-N3 followed by K-N2, R-KR1 and P-KR4 with a dangerous attack.

33 NxN+   RxN
34 Q—Q2   B—KB3
35 Q—Q6   K—N2

36 QxRP?

36 R-K3! is much stronger, defending the bishop before going after Black's QRP. Now Spassky wins material.

36 ...   R—QB1!
37 R—Q6

If 37 B-R1 B-K3 38 BxB RxB 39 Q-R5 B-Q1 and White can resign.

37 ...   RxB
38 RxB(B6)   B—K3!
39 RxB   PxR
40 R—Q1

40 ...   Q—N2?

A time trouble error on the last move of the time control. 40 ... Q-KB1! leaves Black with a winning position because of the mounting pressure on White's king.

41 QxQ   RxQ
42 BxP   RxQRP
43 K—R2   R—R5
44 R—QN1   R—QB2
45 P—B3   R—R3
46 B—N3   R—R6
47 R—N2   R—R8
48 K—N3   K—B3
49 K—N4   R—B6
50 B—Q5   R(R8)—R6
51 P—R4   PxP
52 KxP   R—R8
53 R—Q2   R(R8)—R6
54 K—N4   R—Q6
55 R—K2   R(R6)—B6
56 R—R2   R—R6
57 R—N2

Draw agreed.

White: Spassky
Black: Fischer
Siegen Olympiad, 1970
Grunfeld Defence

1	**P—Q4**	**N—KB3**
2	**P—QB4**	**P—KN3**
3	**N—QB3**	**P—Q4**
4	**PxP**	**NxP**
5	**P—K4**	**NxN**
6	**PxN**	**B—N2**
7	**B—QB4**	**P—QB4**
8	**N—K2**	**N—B3**
9	**B—K3**	**0—0**
10	**0—0**	**Q—B2**
11	**R—B1**	**R—Q1**

12 P—KR3

Varying from the 12 Q-K1 of the first Santa Monica game. The idea of the text is to deprive Black of the use of his KN5 square and to support the eventual advance P-KN4.

12	...	P—N3
13	P—B4	P—K3
14	Q—K1	N—R4
15	B—Q3	P—B4
16	P—N4	PxKP
17	BxP	B—N2
18	N—N3	N—B5

19 BxB

If 19 B-KB2 BxB 20 QxB N-Q7 21 QxKP+ K-R1 22 KR-Q1 N-B6+ 23 K-R1 N-R5! with a fine game for Black who threatens both ... QxP and ... R-K1.

19	...	QxB
20	B—B2	Q—B3
21	Q—K2	PxP
22	PxP	P—QN4
23	N—K4	

23 ...   **BxP**

Weakening the dark squares around his king by exchanging his protecting bishop. Better was 23 ... R-K1 followed by ... QR-Q1 consolidating Black's position in the centre.

24	N—N5	BxB+
25	RxB	R—Q3
26	R—K1	Q—N3
27	N—K4	R—Q5
28	N—B6+	K—R1

28 ... K-N2, although superficially weaker, would have been less unsafe.

29 QxP

29 ...   **R—Q3**

29 ... R-Q8, the move that all the spectators had been expecting, fails to 30 Q-B7 RxR+ 31 K-N2 Q-B3+ 32 K-N3 R-K6+ 33 K-R4 RxP+ 34 KxR Q-R8+ 35 R-R2 Q-KB8+ 36 K-R4 when Black runs out of checks.

30	Q—K4	R—KB1
31	P—N5	R—Q7
32	R(1)—KB1	Q—B2

33	RxR	NxR
34	Q—Q4	R—Q1
35	N—Q5+	K—N1
36	R—B2	N—B5
37	R—K2	R—Q3
38	R—K8+	K—B2
39	R—KB8+!	Resigns

Because of 39 ... KxR 40 Q-R8+ followed by 41 QxP+ and 42 NxQ.

THE SCENE IN REYKJAVIK

The match in Reykjavik is the first match for the World Chess Championship to be held outside Moscow since Botvinnik won the title in 1948. Between 1948 and 1969 no less than ten matches for the title have been played in the Soviet capital, and so the Russians developed a formula for the organization of these events.

The games were usually played on the stage of a large theatre with a seating capacity of several thousands. On the stage would be the table carrying the set, and chairs for the contestants. To one side was another table at which would sit the Chief Referee and his assistant (these have included a Czechoslovak, an Englishman and a Belgian). At the back of the stage was a gigantic demonstration board which showed the position in the current game and also the time taken by the two players.

For some of the matches at least, the spectators in the hall were able to put on earphones and hear a commentary on the game in progress from an eminent grandmaster (there are no shortage of these in Moscow!).

In the foyer of the theatre would be chess book displays and simultaneous exhibitions by top players (in which they would play twenty, thirty or perhaps more opponents at once). Outside, those unable to gain admission (it is rumoured that there was sometimes a black market in tickets) would be able to watch the progress of the game on a second demonstration board even larger than the one on the stage.

These Moscow matches were well covered by Russian radio and television and the games would be reported in all the Soviet newspapers with expert comment. But, except by chess enthusiasts, little attention was paid to these matches by the 'outside' world.

The World Chess Championship is, however, no longer a domestic issue of interest only to the Russians. There is a 'new power in the land' and the Soviet hegemony is severely threatened. This time the outside world was all attention.

What was the set-up in Reykjavik? Broadly, the Icelanders followed the Soviet pattern. Of course they do not have the local grandmasters to call upon (there is just one Icelandic grandmaster, Fridrik Olafsson) but visiting players gave simultaneous displays. There was a large colony of visiting journalists (most of them non-players) and a great many tourist/spectators, something rather rare in the Moscow days. But the biggest change was the presence of an American on the stage!

The Icelanders managed a more up-to-date appearance than the Russians by introducing closed circuit television. Monitors were scattered all around the auditorium showing the players seated at the board. High up at the front of the stage was a large screen which showed the pictures from a second camera. This was trained on the board only and so the audience viewed a gigantic reproduction of the actual pieces instead of the demonstration board idea employed in the Moscow matches.

The match programme provided for three games per week, to be played on Sunday, Tuesday and Thursday from five o'clock to ten in the evening local time. Any game unfinished would then be adjourned and would be played at four p.m the following day. Saturday, Fischer's Sabbath, was a rest day. Each player was allowed a maximum of three postponements on the grounds of illness.

Thus each game had a scheduled first session of five hours. Each player had a clock which recorded his thinking time. When he had made his move he stopped his own clock and this automatically started his opponent's. Each player had two and a half hours in which to make his first forty moves. His clock was fitted with a flag which would drop at the end of his time allowance. If he had not made forty moves when the flag fell then the game would go to his opponent.

Each player was entitled to use his time as he wished but if he spent a lot of time on the early part of the game then he would get into 'time trouble' and would have to hurry with his later moves. If a player was very short of time, a 'time scramble' would occur.

If the game remained unfinished after five hours play, then the player whose turn it was to move had to 'seal' his next move. This means that when he had decided upon his move he would write it on a piece of paper which would be sealed in an envelope and placed in the care of the referee. The other player would not be told this move until the following day when the game would be resumed and the envelope opened.

This strange procedure is adopted for a very good reason. Both players will usually spend many hours working out what to play when the game is continued. The system of sealing a move ensures that neither player can be sure what the position will be on the board when it is next his turn to move. Thus they are placed in an approximately equal position. This is much fairer than simply stopping the game when the player whose turn it was to move would have a whole day in which to work out his best move and would therefore have a great advantage.

To assist him in his study of unfinished games, each player had a second or seconds. Spassky arrived in Iceland with grandmasters Geller and Krogius and International Master Nei while Fischer was helped by grandmaster William Lombardy, an ex-World Junior Champion and now a Jesuit priest. The remainder of the American entourage consisted of Fischer's lawyer, Paul Marshall, and a representative of the United States Chess Federation, Fred Cramer, who might both be classed as trouble-shooters.

Each player received one point for a won game and half a point for a draw. Fischer needed 12½ points to win the title.whereas Spassky needed only twelve points to retain his title but 12½ points to win first prize.

1

Nine long days have preceded this game which should have been played on Sunday, July 2. In the meantime it looked as though the match would never be played. For the first time in its history, chess occupied the headlines on the front pages of the world's press; filling twice as much space as any important political issue like Vietnam.

By Tuesday, July 11, both contestants had seemingly calmed down. Euwe's postponement of this first game had been a reprieve for Fischer and meant that the challenger could feel, after all that had happened, twice as happy. He was presented not only with another chance to play the match, but with double the prize fund as well. His spirits were so high, after his first good sleep in Reykjavik, that he did not even mind reading personally for American TV his repentant letter to Spassky. Bobby's almost boyish sincerity made many people less critical of his previous 'bad manners'. Having received apologies from both Fischer and Dr. Euwe, and after having spent a day or two on a fishing expedition, Spassky also reassumed the confident mood with which he first came to Iceland.

At the drawing of lots, Fischer pointed to Spassky's right hand in which a black pawn was hidden. The exciting question arose of what move Spassky would choose in the first game. While not sharing his challenger's devotion to 1 P-K4, Spassky still likes that move best and used it as his main weapon against Petrosian in 1969. Yet, against Fischer, the champion had preferred 1 P-Q4 on those rare occasions they had met in recent years.

Will Spassky look for his opponent's weaknesses in closed systems again, or will he change his attitude, after eight months of hard preparation, and strike at his most dangerous rival with the king's pawn, expressing a readiness to discuss the sharpest lines which Fischer has analysed for years?

White: Spassky
Black: Fischer
Nimzoindian Defence
    1 P—Q4

Spassky entered the illuminated stage of the large tournament hall a minute before five p.m. Icelandic time. Fischer was not there. So, all the initial applause of thousands of spectators (the Soviet ambassador was also noticed there) went to the title holder. The Icelandic referee pushed the clock. (Chief Referee, grandmaster Lothar Schmid, returned later from his home in Germany where his son had been involved in a slight accident). The silence was automatically established and Spassky, after a short while (perhaps waiting for his opponent to appear), made his first move.

An atmosphere of some tension was created and nine minutes had elapsed before Fischer finally arrived, shook hands with the champion, and made his move without much reflection.

    1 ...   N—KB3
    2 P—QB4   P—K3

A solid and rather cautious approach to the first game of the match.

    3 N—KB3

The same remark goes for Spassky, who sends an invitation for the Queen's Indian Defence, but in vain . . .

    3 ...   P—Q4
    4 N—B3   B—N5

Offering the possibility of the Nimzo-indian Defence once more. The move in the game is more aggressive and therefore perhaps more to Fischer's taste than the modest 4 ... B-K2. The American grand-master used to play 4 ... P-B4, but Spassky showed the right strategy against that move in the fifth game of his match with Petrosian in 1969: 5 BPxP NxP 6 P-K4 NxN 7 PxN PxP 8 PxP B-N5+ 9 B-Q2 BxB+ 10 QxB 0-0 11 B-B4 N-B3 12 0-0 P-QN3 13 QR-Q1 B-N2 14 KR-K1 R-B1 15 P-Q5! and White's passed QP won the day.

5   P-K3

Only now, White agrees to transpose into a position from the Nimzoindian Defence. What is the idea? White has, with the different order of moves, avoided the sharper lines after 1 P-Q4 N-KB3 2 P-QB4 P-K3 3 N-QB3 B-N5 4 P-K3 e.g. 4 ... P-QN3 or 4 ... P-B4.

The alternatives 5 Q-R4+ and 5 B-N5 would be a less classical and less clear choice, while 5 PxP could lead to simpli-fications too early.

5	...	0-0
6	B-Q3	P-B4
7	0-0	N-B3
8	P-QR3	

It seems that this well known position suited both player's preparations.

8   ...   B-R4

Not recognized as best, and thus a small surprise to Spassky who now began to think for the first time in the game. Larsen's intermediate move 8...QPxP or the classical 8...BxN are more frequently played.

9   N-K2

The 'red book' (the collection of 355 of Spassky's games edited by Dr. Wildhagen in Hamburg) which, according to American newspapers was in Fischer's hands all the time during his preparations for the match and even during meals, does its job! Spassky, probably not too well acquainted with the crucial variations, repeats an unpretentious continuation of fourteen years ago. The psychological judgement of the challenger is a very daring one, as it follows a game between Spassky and Krogius — Krogius was now a member of the champion's team in Reykjavik.

A more ambitious attempt in my opinion would be not to waste a move on a deve-loped piece and thus avoid the pressure of Black's KB, but to fight for the pair of bishops and the centre with 9 BPxP KPxP 10 PxP BxN 11 PxB e.g. 11 ... B-N5 12 P-B4 P-Q5!? 13 R-N1! with advantage to White. Gligoric-Szabo, Beverwijk 1967.

The move in the game escapes theore-tical, elaborated routes and threatens 10 QPxP, but Black first has the option to simplify.

Was Spassky to be blamed for his choice? Fischer has never before tried this line, which has appeared only few times in tournament praxis in the last few years. Who, unprepared for it, could forecast what Fischer had up his sleeve?

9   ...   QPxP

Less double-edged than 9 ... BPxP 10 KPxP PxP 11 BxBP P-KR3 12 B-R2 (or 12 B-B4 P-R3 13 R-B1 N-K2 14 B-R2 B-Q2 15 B-K5 N(2)-Q4 with a good game, Petrosian-Tolush, USSR 1951) 12 ... B-B2 13 N-B3 N-K2 14 R-K1 P-QN3 Hodos-Krogius, 30th USSR Championship, 1960.

10   BxBP   B-N3

Defending the pawn and removing the bishop from an exposed square.

11   PxP

Otherwise, White would have to put up with an isolated pawn in the centre. Black now takes the opportunity to enter an even endgame, for he has no weaknesses in his position.

11   ...   QxQ

More radical now than later.

The Spassky-Krogius game went

11...BxP 12 P-QN4 QxQ (Weaker is 12...B-Q3 13 B-N2 P-K4 14 N-N3 Q-K2 15 Q-B2! B-N5 16 QR-Q1 P-KN3 17 B-K2 QR-B1 18 Q-N1 when White has a clear plus. Gasztonyi-Dely, Hungary 1966) 13 RxQ B-K2, transposing back to the present game.

12	RxQ	BxP
13	P—QN4	B—K2
14	B—N2	B—Q2

The prepared (?) improvement and the little trick which shows that Black has no difficulties in completing his development (15 BxN? BxB 16 RxB?? BxR). White was probably remembering and hoping that he might make something of this endgame: 14...P-QN3?! 15 N-B4 B-N2 16 N-N5 N-Q1 17 QR-B1 P-KR3? 18 N(5)xKP! PxN 19 NxP R-B1 20 B-N3 N-B2 21 NxR KxN 22 RxR+ BxR 23 R-QB1 N-Q3 24 P-B3 N(B3)-K1 25 P-K4 B-N4 26 P-B4! BxP 27 R-B1 P-KN4 28 P-N3 B-R6 29 R-B2 NxP 30 R-K2 N-Q7 31 PxB NxB 32 R-K3 and White won in 50 moves (Spassky-Krogius, 25th USSR Championship, Riga 1958).

15 QR—B1

15 N(2)-Q4 appears to be more precise.

15 ...   KR—Q1

16 N(2)—Q4

This knight was passive on K2 and therefore White offers to exchange it. 16 N-B3 would avoid the simplification, but, at the same time, White would not achieve much bringing the knight back to where it was before with a loss of a tempo.

16 ...   NxN

17 NxN

After 17 BxN B-R5 White would not be able to cover the QR4-Q1 diagonal, but 17 RxN was also playable. The game now enters a peaceful harbour, but neither of the players would risk the offer of a draw for the sake of his prestige.

17 ...   B-R5

Using the hole on White's queen side to activate his pieces more quickly.

18 B—N3   BxB

18...RxN? 19 BxB serves no purpose. The exchange of light squared bishops favours Black, for White is a litttle weak on the light squares on the queen side and his pawns there are slightly exposed.

19 NxB   RxR+

A small gain in time for Black, because

White has, by now, moved both rooks in order to have only one left on Q1.

20 RxR   R—QB1

Trying to say that the QB-file is a more precious one than the Q-file to White's rook, where all possible penetration squares are protected by Black.

21 K—B1

Bringing the king closer to the area of potential danger.

21 ...   K—B1

Black also activates his king. 21...R-B7 is no threat because of 22 R-Q2.

22 K—K2   N—K5

The first serious threat in the game: 23 ... R-B7+ and wins. White has nothing better than his next move.

23 R—QB1   RxR

24 BxR

Better than 24 NxR, as White also has something to say with an eventual N-R5.

24 ...   P—B3

With the purpose of protecting the defensive square Q3 for the black knight from any attack by White's bishop.

25 N—R5   N—Q3

Black must not weaken the structure of his pawns, as they would be exposed to further attacks by White's knight without there being any possibility to defend them well.

26 K—Q3   B—Q1

Chasing the more active of his opponent's pieces away without making committal pawn moves.

27 N—B4   B—B2

Activating the bishop at the same time.

28 NxN   BxN

29 P—N5

Removing pawns from black squares and thereby leaving all his worries behind.

29 ...   BxKRP?

Let us quote something from Norman Mailer's book 'Cannibals and Christians' about Scranton in his try for President: 'One felt he had been spoiled when he was young by a lack of testing. It was not that he lacked bravery, it was that he had lacked all opportunity to be brave for much too long, and now he was not so much engaged in a serious political struggle as in a puberty rite.'

Was it lack of serious resistance to Fischer in his previous qualification matches which made the challenger feel over confident at this moment and ripe to make the worst blunder in his whole chess career (if he ever made one before?). Was it a vain wish to show his opponent that he cannot get half a point that easily, or just the prejudice that with the capture of a pawn Black was crowning his (non-existent) 'initiative'?

The move in the game is a hardly believable oversight in an entirely drawish position, adding drama to a tranquil and rather monotonous beginning to the match. Surprisingly, Black took very little time to decide on such a dangerous continuation. Had Fischer thought for a few minutes more, and another move ahead, he would easily have realised that after 30 P-N3 P-KR4 31 K-K2 P-R5 32 K-B3 P-R6 33 K-N4 B-N8 34 KxP BxP White has the intermediate move 35 B-Q2, finally closing the cage on the black piece.

30 P—N3   P—KR4
31 K—K2   P—R5
32 K—B3

An impulse caused by Black's impatience and levity, not compatible with Fischer's true chess character, probably made him believe for a while that here White was forced to accept a worse pawn structure with 32 PxP.

32 ...   K—K2

It did not take long for Fischer to realize his terrible mistake, but he kept his head cool. The move in the game looked like the best chance for some counterplay now. Yet, the strange continuation 32...P-N4 33

K-N2 P-N5 34 KxB P-R6 could have been an interesting practical chance, too.

33 K—N2   PxP
34 PxP   BxP
35 KxB   K—Q3

Is there any chance, thanks to the active black king, to save the end game having only two pawns for the unnecessarily lost piece?

36 P—QR4

The best. White had to avoid being left with the QR pawn, e.g. 36 P-K4 K-B4 37 B-K3+ KxP 38 BxP K-B5 with chances for a draw because the RP queens on a square of the wrong colour for the bishop: 39 K-B3 K-Q6 threatening P-K4 and P-N4-N5+. Also, 36 K-N4 P-KN3 37 B-N2 P-K4 could not do much for White.

36 ...   K—Q4

Better than 36 ... K-B4 37 B-R3+. Now, Black keeps open the possibility for his king to go to either side.

37 B—R3   K—K5

It looks like an important advantage for Black to have his king on that central, dominant square, and White had no time to prevent it. In case of 37 ... P-QR3 or 37 ... P-QN3 White can operate very well with the threatened B-B8 at the proper moment, opening the access of White's king to the black pawns.

38 B—B5   P—QR3

Not 38...P-QN3 39 BxP! PxB 40 P-R5 and wins.

39 P—N6!

White has to keep as many pawns on the board as possible in order to diminish his opponent's chances for a draw.

39 ...   P—B4

If 39 ... P-K4 40 K-N4 P-N3 41 B-K7 KxP 42 BxP P-K5 43 K-N5 K-Q6 44 KxP K-B5 45 K-B5 the position would be similar to the one in the game after the adjournment.

40 K—R4   P—B5?

This destroys the last chance for a draw by making his own passed pawns less dangerous. After 40...K-Q4 41 B-Q4 P-K4 42 B-B3 K-K5 43 K-N5 P-B5 44 PxP PxP or 41 B-K7 K-K5 42 B-N5 P-K4 and P-B5, Black's king will run to the queen side saving the game. With the move in the game Black only temporarily cuts his opponent's king off from the play, thus achieving nothing.

White decided to adjourn the game, seal his obvious 41st move and sacrifice about 25 minutes on his clock because five hours of play had not been completed at that moment. In home analysis the road to victory was to be found in full safety.

41 PxP   KxP

42 K—R5

This is the right method: White tries to get closer to the Queen side and to decide the game there. Very wrong would be 42 B-Q6+ P-K4 43 P-R5?, because Black would reach a stalemate position by heading his king to QR1 or QB1 whichever was allowed.

42 ...   K—B4

Black prevents White's king from entering play, as 42 ... P-N4 43 K-N6 P-N5 44 K-B6 P-K4 45 B-Q6 would win easily.

43 B—K3   K—K5
44 B—B2

The key! White keeps the bishop on the best diagonal where it protects his winning chance, the QN pawn, and controls the advance of both of Black's passed pawns.

44 ...   K—B4

A must, again.

45 B—R4!

Forcing Black to move a pawn and aiming to create a 'zugzwang' position.

45 ...   P—K4

46 B—N5   P—K5
47 B—K3

Coming back to the best diagonal after having completed the first task. Now, Black has no useful move and must allow his opponent's king out of its temporary prison.

47 ...   K—B3
48 K—N4   K—K4
49 K—N5   K—Q4

Black has no other choice.

50 K—B5

Of course, always closer to the centre and to the queen side.

50 ...   P—R4

50...K-B5 51 KxP K-N5 52 K-Q5 KxP 53 K-Q6 wins. So, Black makes his last attempt to gain a tempo for the later race on the queen side.

51 B—B2

Continuing to insist on the established 'zugzwang.'

51 ...   P—N4

The only weapon left to distract White's king from the crucial area.

52 KxNP   K—B5

Now—or never.

53 K—B5   K—N5
54 KxP   KxP
55 K—Q5   K—N4
56 K—Q6

Black resigns. White's king comes to QB7 and decides the issue.

The score 1:0 to Spassky.

2

Did hidden TV cameras remind Fischer of human eyes, staring constantly at him and distracting his attention from the chess board? Whatever the reason the choice 'Cameras, or me?' offered by Fischer on the eve of the second game, put the Icelandic organizers and the American firm of Mr. Chester Fox (which had bought all filming rights) in a state of disbelief.

Was not the American grandmaster the one who fought stubbornly for several months for his and Spassky's right each to receive thirty per cent of the income from television? Did he wish to throw all that income away (the organizers did not, for 60,000 dollars had been spent on the preparations for the match), and not only that, but an excellent share of the prize fund of 250,000 dollars if he left the match unfinished? Common sense said: 'No, it would not be possible.' Can a 'whim' be more precious than some two hundred thousand?

The cameras remained (it was in the contract, agreed by the players). So did Bobby. But in his hotel room. Twenty five minutes before the forfeit, Mr. Fox, in desperation, sent a message by telephone from the tournament hall that the cameras would be removed if only Fischer would be willing to come and play. Then the challenger also wanted the thirty five minutes back on his clock. But there are playing rules. So, that could only be done if ever-moving time could be turned back. No-one could do it, not even for the sake of the match.

Fischer lost by forfeit because the leader of the white pieces failed to appear during the first hour of play. As a matter of fact, he did not appear on that day at all but remained locked in his room with the telephone plug pulled out.

Score: 2:0 for Spassky.

3

Was the match off, or was it on? At eight o'clock in the morning, Fischer delivered his letter of protest personally to the referee, Lothar Schmid, as he had done with the letter to Spassky before the match began. The German grandmaster, surprised in his room and still in his pyjamas, hit the low hanging lamp with his head. Realizing that his unexpected presence was the cause, Bobby said: 'Very, very, sorry!' He was polite and extremely kind. The written protest against the forfeit was less so. Was Fischer going to withdraw as he did, for similar reasons, during the Sousse Interzonal of 1967?

The Tournament Committee turned the protest down. Its members also inspected the hall and found 'that playing conditions in every respect conformed to the Match Rules and that all likely sources of disturbance were well controlled.' In the meantime, Spassky went fishing for salmon to get away from it all.

Very few people expected Fischer to come on that Sunday to the tournament hall and continue the match. Probably, neither did Spassky. If Fischer's reasoning was rational rather than emotional, he would take the only correct decision instead of risking not only so much money but also his reputation. But, as he had not appeared on Thursday, thereby giving away a point without any fight on the board, could he behave differently three days later when in an even worse situation in the match?

Fischer was rumoured to have booked a flight from Reykjavik to Greenland but it turned out to be a German tourist with the same name. Yet it was true that he had reserved a seat to New York on the day of the third game (Fischer called it the second). Two hours before the game was due to begin, Fischer's lawyer Paul Marshall and his second William Lombardy called the referee and asked, on behalf of Fischer, the favour that the game be played in a room behind the stage. That call produced a chance of a compromise. Schmid called Spassky and the champion generously agreed. But later, Spassky almost changed his mind and wanted to play in the main hall when his challenger, instead of sitting at the table and starting the game, began to talk about the camera switching on and off. Schmid himself stopped the clock and saved the situation during an unprecedented delay of eight minutes.

A closed circuit camera (the only one which did not disturb the challenger) reproduced the game on a big screen in the main hall. Instead of the game itself the spectators watched an exciting soundless replica.

To Spassky's 1 P-Q4 Fischer hesitated to give his reply. From time to time he turned in his black swivel armchair (the same type as he had used in Buenos Aires) to the referee and complained about something (was it the colour of the pieces, which denoted that the second game was irrevocably over?). Five minutes elapsed before Fischer decided to make his first move. He could not hear the applause in the hall, which signified the sigh of relief among the crowd. Once more, the 'greatest sports event' was saved.

White: Spassky
Black: Fischer
Modern Benoni

1 P—Q4	N—KB3
2 P—QB4	P—K3
3 N—KB3	P—B4

This is much sharper than 3...P-Q4 as played in the first game of the match.

4 P—Q5

The champion accepts the challenge for an open fight. Was it a tactical mistake? Perhaps Spassky decided that as his opponent had not walked out of the match, he would try to put him out of it as quickly as possible. Or did Fischer's once more unexpected arrival produce another switch of psychological advantage from Spassky to his opponent?

4 ...	PxP
5 PxP	P—Q3
6 N—B3	P—KN3
7 N—Q2	

The so called semi-Benoni could not come as a surprise to Spassky, and in his preparations he had probably evolved some reason for this move instead of the more frequently played 7 P-K4.

7 ...	QN—Q2

Being ready to meet the positional threat 8 N-B4 and 9 B-B4 with 8....N-N3. e.g. 8 N-B4 N-N3 9 P-K4 NxN 10 BxN B-N2 11 0-0 0-0 12 B-B4 P-QR3 13 P-QR4 N-R4! with equal chances. Gligoric-Trifunovic, Yugoslav Championship 1957. 8 P-KN3 also leads to an even game: 8 ... B-N2 9 B-N2 0-0 10 0-0 Q-K2 11 N-B4 N-K4 12 NxN QxN. Gligoric-Petrosian, Zurich 1953.

8 P—K4	B—N2
9 B—K2	0—0
10 0—0	R—K1

Transposing into a well-known position. The specific order of moves chosen by White deprived his opponent of the possibility to play one of the other lines e.g. with QN-R3 or B-KN5, if he ever intended to do so.

11 Q—B2

A prepared novelty? It has the good intention to save a tempo for White's development, but, at the same time, it somehow removes the queen from the defence of the king side. Another possibility is 11 P-QR4 (weaker is 11 P-B3 P-QR3 12 P-QR4 Q-B2 13 Q-N3?! N-K4 14 P-R5 R-N1 15 N-Q1 N-R4 16 N-B4 P-B4 17 PxP BxP! 18 P-N4 NxN 19 BxN P-QN4 20 PxP e.p. RxNP 21 Q-R2 B-Q5+ 22 K-N2 Q-KN2! with advantage to Black. Tukmakov-Tal, 37th USSR Championship 1969) and now;

1) 11 ... P-QR3: 1a) 12 P-B4! (12 P-B3 would transpose into Tukmakov-Tal, quoted above) 12 ... P-B5! 13 P-K5! PxP 14 NxP N-N3 15 PxP N-N5! 16 N-Q6! BxP 17 NxR BxP+? (17 ... Q-R5! leads to interesting complications) 18 K-R1 Q-R5 19 B-KN5! QxB 20 BxN and White won. Gligoric-Nicevski, Rovinj 1970;

1b) 12 P-R5 P-QN4 13 PxP e.p. NxNP 14 P-B3 Q-B2 15 N-B4 KN-Q2 16 B-Q2 NxN 17 BxN N-N3 18 P-N3 with an even game. Gligoric-Minic, Rovinj 1970;

1c) 12 Q-B2 P-N3 (or 12...R-N1. Purdy-Hartoch, Siegen 1970) 13 P-B4 R-N1 14 R-N1 (better 14 K-R1) P-B5! 15 K-R1 P-QN4 16 PxP PxP with strong counterplay. Fernandez-Velimirovic, Havana 1971;

1d) 12 R-K1 R-N1 13 B-B1 N-K4 14 P-B4? (14 P-R3) N(4)-N5 15 N-B3 (15 P-R3 NxQP!) P-B5! 16 P-R5 Q-B2 17 P-K5 (Donner-Velimirovic, Havana 1971) and Black missed a win with 17 ... PxP 18 PxP B-B1!;

Or 2) 11 ... N-K4 12 Q-B2 P-KN4;

2a) 13 N-B3 NxN+ 14 BxN P-KR3 (Gligoric-Fischer, Palma de Mallorca 1970), but the easiest way to equalise was 14 ... N-Q2 15 B-N4 N-K4 16 BxB RxB;

2b) 13 N-B4 NxN 14 BxN N-N5 15 N-K2! P-QR3 16 R-R3 Q-K2 17 R-KN3! P-R3 18 P-B4! QxP 19 B-Q3 Q-N5 20 PxP PxP 21 BxNP QxNP 22 QxQ BxQ 23 R-B4 R-K6 (Najdorf-Ree, Wijk aan Zee 1971) and White missed the win by 24 R(4)-B3! RxR 25 PxR N-K4 26 B-B6+ K-B1 27 B-R7 K-K1 28 R-N8+ K-Q2 29 B-B5+ K-B2 30 B-Q8+ K-N1 31 B-QN6.

2c) 13 P-QN3! P-N5! 14 B-N2 N-R4 with chances for both sides. Gligoric-Tatai, Venice 1971.

11 ...   N—R4!

Exploiting the absence of white's queen from the Q1-KR5 diagonal, Black seizes his best chance for active counterplay.

12 BxN

What else? 12 P-KN3 N-K4 or 12 N-B4 N-K4 brings White nowhere; and 12 P-B4 would dangerously open the position of White's king.

12 ...   PxB
13 N—B4   N—K4
14 N—K3

Taking better control over the hole on KB5.

14 ...   Q—R5!

Creating unpleasant threats around his opponent's king.

15 B—Q2

Improving his development and waiting for Black to declare his intentions.

15 ...   N-N5

A strictly positional solution. 15 ... B-Q2 was also playable, but 15 ... N-B6+?! was not sound enough: 16 PxN B-K4 17 KR-B1 creating an escape route for the king via KB1.

16 NxN   PxN

Correcting the pawn formation again.

17 B-B4

There is nothing better than to take this important diagonal, yet, White had to spend two moves to get the bishop to this square.

17 ...   Q—B3!

The more pieces on the board, the easier it is for Black to keep plenty of counterplay. In contrast, 17 ... B-K4 would give White an easy game.

18 P—KN3

An important decision, which makes a lasting weakness out of his KP. White had to try 18 B-N3 (18...P-KR4 19 P-B3).

18 ...   B—Q2
19 P—QR4   P—N3!

Making the chain of pawns intact. Now Black has a clear plan, pressure along the K-file, and a flexible pawn majority on the queen side.

20 KR—K1   P—QR3

An obvious confirmation that Black's majority of pawns on the queen side has more value than White's preponderance on the opposite wing.

21 R—K2

Looking for his best chance to break through with P-K5, if it becomes possible.

21 ...   P—N4
22 QR—K1

22 PxP PxP 23 RxR RxR 24 P-K5 R-R8+ 25 K-N2 PxP 26 RxP P-N5 27 N-K4 Q-QR3 would not be pleasant for White.

22 ...   Q—N3

Meeting the threat of P-K5 and putting the queen on her ideal square.

23 P—N3

Black is stronger on the queen side, so White intends not to open the position in that area but somehow to block Black's mass of pawns.

23 ...   R—K2

Black has more to say in this position.

24 Q—Q3   R—N1
25 PxP

White has to think of the threat P-B5.

25 ...   PxP
26 P—N4

Black's pawns had to be blocked, otherwise, 26 ... P-N5 and 27 ... B-N4 would follow.

26 ...   P—B5

Black trades the blockade of the queen side for the strategic gain of a passed pawn. He has good reason for it, since if 26...PxP 27 N-R2 R-QB1 28 NxP R-B5 29 N-B6 White could hold on quite well.

27 Q—Q2   R(1)—K1

The crisis in the game approaches its climax. Is White able to defend? Not 28 B-N5? because of 28...BxN.

28 R—K3   P—R4

Giving an additional escape to the king. 28...BxN 29 RxP RxP 30 RxR RxR 31 RxR QxR would offer nothing because of 32 Q-B6! B-B4 33 Q-N5+ B-N3 34 B-Q2.

29 R(3)—K2

White has no better choice than to wait and leave it to his opponent to show what Black can do.

29 ...   K—R2

Black tests his opponent's patience and hesitates for a while in making his own decision.

30 R—K3   K—N1
31 R(3)—K2

The repetition of moves suited White well, for he had less time up to the time control. Seeing no other way to break through, Black decides to exchange bishop for knight in order to win a pawn.

31	...	BxN
32	QxB	RxP
33	RxR	RxR

34 RxR

This exchange makes the black queen mightier. Yet, 34 R-R1 R-K1 was not attractive either (35 R-R6? Q-N8+ 36 K-N2 R-K8 37 R-R8+ B-K1), and Black could even try playing the endgame with an eventual Q-Q6.

34 ...   QxR
35 B—R6

Not 35 BxP? QxP 36 Q-B6 Q-Q8+ 37 K-N2 B-B3+ and wins.

35 ...   Q—N3
36 B—B1   Q—N8
37 K—B1

Wishing to get out of the cage. White is cramped and therefore Black's attack on the light squares is stronger than any counteraction by White on the dark squares.

37 ...   B—B4
38 K—K2   Q—K5+

Black forces White's queen to leave the long diagonal. Very wrong would be 38 ... B-K5 39 B-N2 B-B6+ 40 K-Q2! Q-Q8+ 41 K-K3 Q-K7+ 42 K-B4 Q-K5+ 43 K-N5 QxP+ 44 K-R6 K-B1 45 Q-R8+ K-K2 46 B-B6+ K-K3 47 K-N7! and White's queen is ready for numerous and inescapable checks.

39 Q—K3   Q—B7+

39 ... QxP? 40 Q-N5+ would be a draw.

40 Q—Q2?

Paying the debt to his opponent who, also, made the decisive mistake in time trouble, and on the 40th move, in the first game of the match. After 40 K-K1 White would still have hopes to live.

40 ...   Q—N6

It looks terrible for White, but still 41 K-K1 could offer resistance. Instead, the time approached to adjourn the game. White hastened with his move in order to make Fischer seal.

41 Q—Q4?

Out of premature desperation, seeing that 41 B-N2 Q-B6+ 42 K-K1 Q-R8+ 43 K-K2 B-Q6+ loses immediately. This makes things easy for Black who took little time to find the killing move and put it in the envelope.

What if 41 ... B-Q6+ 42 K-K3 Q-Q8?

See diagram next page.

41   ...   B—Q6+!

White resigns (on the next day after having seen the best sealed move). The first victory over Spassky in Fischer's chess career!

Fischer arrived a quarter of an hour late for the adjourned session at the tournament hall and missed being congratulated by the champion who found it discomforting to wait for too long with the clock stopped.

The score: 2:1 to Spassky.

4

After the adjournment of the third game Spassky made no protest, just a simple statement that he would not play in the back room again. The referees agreed with the champion. When built, the spacious room had been intended for table tennis. During those five hours of playing chess there it was discovered that all kinds of outside noise could be heard: traffic on the road above, cars in the parking lot, children playing on the near-by grounds.

What about Fischer? A friend remarked: 'That was the right kind of noise. Not like that from cameras.' This makes sense. In certain countries which are less touched by Western civilisation, people do not agree to be photographed! Fischer was not acting. His dislike for cameras was in-born; a genuine one. There were years of his solitary life when not one recent photo of Bobby could be found for the press.

The tournament committee used instruments to measure the noise in the main playing hall. There was none. Yet if Fischer could not hear the cameras, he could sense them. The challenger preferred the isolation from cameras and public to the isolation from the sounds in the street. So he let his representative write a letter pointing out that the Committee's conclusion about 'all sources of disturbance being well controlled in the main hall' was not accurate. The members of the Committee noticed, with relief, that the letter was not signed by Fischer himself. According to the match regulations this gave them the right to disregard it.

But a hidden fear grew among the officials. What would happen that afternoon when the players were due to meet in the main hall for the fourth game? Would Fischer once more insist on moving to the room behind the stage and thus possibly ruin the match?

No, the challenger kept quiet! After all, the room behind also had a closed circuit camera to reproduce the game for the spectators on a big screen in the hall. To that camera Fischer never objected. But perhaps he remembered the impossible situation before the third game, which caused the delay of eight minutes. While showing the progress of the game on a magnified, illuminated chess diagram, the camera would switch from time to time to the players.

Fischer wanted to know when it was off and when it was on them, but the lentil on the wall of the ping-pong room always looked the same and did not say. The only way out was for the camera crew to shout when the camera was off, and when it was on, in order to instruct the players how to behave. Not only Fischer but Spassky as well, refused to accept the suggestion.

Perhaps the American grandmaster was influenced by a flood of supporting telegrams organized in a steady flow by chess friends in the United States who were trying to persuade him to play during the crisis before the third game? Or was it the long-distance call from Kissinger in Washington (at about the same time) that made Bobby feel differently? (Some people even suggested that Fischer's premature departure could provoke a domestic movement in Iceland to force out the American military base.) Well . . .

Anyhow, there were none of the usual complications surrounding the fourth game. That Tuesday evening after the game, when at dinner in his hotel, the patient referee grandmaster Lothar Schmid was seen in a bright mood for the first time. Were the committee meetings over?

White: Fischer
Black: Spassky
Sicilian Defence

| 1 | P—K4 | P—QB4! |

A surprise. In moments of great responsibility Spassky always used to stick to the classical 1 ... P-K4, as he did against Fischer in the second Piatagorsky Cup in Santa Monica and at the Olympiad in Havana, 1966.

2	N—KB3	P—Q3
3	P—Q4	PxP
4	NxP	N—KB3
5	N—QB3	N—B3
6	B—QB4	

Fischer's all-round weapon against the Sicilian Defence. Spassky must have expected it.

| 6 | ... | P—K3 |
| 7 | B—N3 | |

Eliminating the danger of Black's ... NxP followed by ... P-Q4.

| 7 | ... | B—K2 |
| 8 | B—K3 | |

Avoiding 8 0-0 NxN 9 QxN 0-0 10 P-B4 P-QN3 11 K-R1 B-R3! 12 R-B3 P-Q4 13 PxP B-B4 14 Q-R4 B-N2 15 B-K3 PxP 16 B-Q4 (Fischer-Geller, Curacao 1962) when 16 ... P-QR3 would have offered good chances to Black.

| 8 | ... | 0—0 |

Weaker is 8 ... P-QR3 9 P-B4 Q-B2 10 0-0 N-QR4 11 Q-B3 0-0 12 P-B5 P-K4 13 N(4)-K2 NxB 14 RPxN P-QN4 15 P-KN4 P-N5 16 P-N5!, Fischer-Hamann, Natanya 1968.

| 9 | 0—0 | |

Fischer tried the unclear continuation 9 Q-K2 and 10 0-0-0 against Geller (Skopje 1967) and Larsen (Palma de Mallorca 1970) without any success.

Premature would be 9 P-B4 NxN 10 BxN P-QN4! 11 P-K5 PxP 12 PxP N-Q2

13 0-0 P-QR3 (or 13 ... B-B4! 14 BxB NxB 15 QxQ KRxQ 16 NxP B-R3 17 B-B4 QR-N1 18 P-QR4 NxP! with equality. Fischer-Geller, Curacao 1962) 14 N-K4 B-N2 15 Q-N4 (or 15 N-Q6 BxN 16 PxB Q-N4 17 Q-K2 QR-Q1 18 QR-Q1 P-K4 19 B-K3 Q-N3 with counterplay) 15 ... BxN 16 QxB N-B4 with the better game for Black. Klovski-Shamkovich, USSR 1971.

| 9 | ... | P—QR3 |

After eight months of preparation Spassky was bound to know what he was doing, for Fischer has played more than twenty tournament games with this line, and crushed many opponents. For instance:

1) 9 ... N-QR4 10 P-B4 P-QN3 11 P-K5 N-K1 12 P-B5 QPxP 13 PxP NxB 14 N-B6 Q-Q3 15 QxQ BxQ 16 RPxN BxP 17 NxRP with the better endgame. Fischer-Korchnoi, Curacao 1962;

2) 9 ... B-Q2 10 P-B4 NxN (Interesting is 10 ... Q-B1. Fischer-Larsen, fifth match game, Denver 1971) 11 BxN B-B3 12 Q-K2 P-QN4 13 NxP and now:

2a) 13 ... BxP 14 NxRP P-K4 15 PxP PxP 16 B-K3 Q-N1 17 N-N5 B-B3 18 N-B3 with a material advantage. Fischer-Saidy, East Orange 1957;

2b) 13 ... BxN 14 QxB NxP 15 P-B5 B-B3 16 Q-Q3 P-Q4 17 BxB NxB 18 P-B4 QPxP 19 QxQ KRxQ 20 BxP with the better endgame. Fischer-Weinstein, USA Championship 1958/59.

3) 9 ... NxN 10 BxN P-QN4!? 11 NxNP B-R3 12 P-QB4 BxN 13 PxB NxP 14 Q-N4 N-B3 15 Q-K2 N-Q2 (Fischer-Korchnoi, Rovinj 1970), and now White missed the best continuation 16 QR-B1.

10   P—B4   NxN

Passive is 10 ... B-Q2 11 P-B5! Q-B1? 12 PxP BxP 13 NxB PxN 14 N-R4! (Fischer-Larsen, third match game, Denver 1971).

11   BxN   P—QN4
12   P—QR3

Or 12 Q-B3 B-N2 13 P-QR3 P-QR4! 14 QR-K1 P-N5 15 PxP PxP 16 N-N1 P-Q4 17 PxP BxP 18 BxB PxB 19 P-B3 N-K5 20 R-Q1 P-B4 with advantage to Black. Radulov-Bobotzov, Bulgaria 1967.

12   ...   B—N2
13   Q—Q3

A well known type of position. In the game Nikolayevsky-Geller, USSR Championship 1959, Black, in a very similar position, played the passive Q-B2.

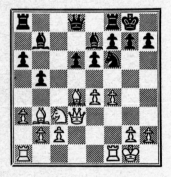

13   ...   P—QR4!?

A prepared improvement. Black is ready to meet the positional threat 14 P-B5 with 14 ... P-N5 followed by ... P-K4 after White's knight has been driven away from the centre. In fact Black MUST continue with his queen side action without any loss of time.

14   P—K5

White is almost forced to alter his strategy. Removing the pawn from the attacked square White challenges the correctness of Black's offered pawn sacrifice.

14   ...   PxP
15   PxP   N—Q2
16   NxP   N—B4

This obviously ought to be a position which has been analyzed by the Soviet team at home.

17   BxN

Wasting no time on any retreat of the queen and keeping the light squared bishop on the board as this gives better protection to White's queen side. Also, after the inevitable 17 ... NxB White would have difficulties in overcoming various tactical threats.

17   ...   BxB+
18   K—R1

Is there sufficient compensation for a pawn? After having spent only 5 minutes on the whole opening (Fischer used half an hour), Spassky now began to think for a long time.

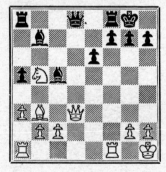

18   ...   Q—N4

An ambitious move, which gives to the game more excitement than just a dull striving for a draw after 18 ... QxQ (cutting White's mass of pawns in two parts) 19 PxQ B-R3 20 N-B7 R-R2 21 NxB RxN 22 B-B4 R-R2, although it could be sufficient for Spassky to split the point in view of his lead in the match.

19   Q—K2

A safer alternative was 19 Q-N3, but White prefers to have his queen centralised underestimating the dangers in this position.

19	...	QR—Q1
20	QR—Q1	RxR
21	RxR	

A sign that Black had created new problems for himself was the times on the clock. By now Spassky had spent longer on his moves than Fischer.

21 ...   P—R4!

Black's best chance by far is to go for action against the opponent's king. It could have been done equally efficiently by 21 ... B-K6! 22 N-Q6 B-B3 23 N-B4 B-B5 24 K-N1 P-QR5 25 B-R2 P-R4, or 22 N-Q4 QxKP 23 N-B3 Q-B5 leaving White in a hopeless situation.

Black had nothing to do on the Q-file: 21 ... R-Q1? 22 N-Q6.

22 N—Q6   B—R1

With the exchange of a pair of rooks, Black has left this square free for the bishop and diminished White's pressure along the KB-file.

23 B—B4

White is still confident and plays coolly and rather quickly, preparing the centralisation of his passive bishop, and making the road free for his QN-pawn.

23 ...   P—KR5

Probably only now did White realize that he is exposed to a severe attack and Fischer began to think. Spassky's whole continuation had not just been bluff!

24 P—R3

He must stop the threat of 24 ... P-R6.

24 ...   B—K6

Black plays for a win! The other possibility was 24 ... Q-N6 25 N-K4 (not 25 R-Q3? because of 25 ... BxP+! 26 QxB Q-K8+

27 K-R2 QxP+ 28 K-R1 Q-K8+ 29 K-R2 BxN+ 30 RxB Q-K4+ winning the rook) 25 ... QxKP 26 NxB QxN establishing material equality.

25 Q—N4

25 R-Q3 B-B5 would leave White's pieces in an awkward position, and the deadly threat 25 ... Q-N6 had to be prevented.

25 ...   QxP?

Missing a golden opportunity: 25 ... QxQ 26 PxQ B-B5 27 R-K1 P-R6 28 B-B1 P-B3 29 N-B4 PxP, and if 30 NxRP? B-N6 31 R-Q1 RxB+ etc.

26 QxRP

26 NxP?! was not correct because of 26 ... KxN! and Black's king would reach safety on either K2 or KR1.

26 ...   P—N4

Fighting sharply for the square Q1 for his rook and KN6 for his queen. Also playable was 26 ... B-N4.

27 Q—N4

Preventing 27 ... Q-N6 and 28 ... B-B5.

27 ...   B—B4

Black realized that 27 ... R-Q1 could not win because of 28 NxP! RxR+ 29 QxR Q-K5 (or 29 ... Q-N6 30 N-R6+! K-N2 31 Q-Q7+ with perpetual check) 30 B-B1 KxN 31 Q-Q7+ K-B3 32 Q-Q8+ K-K4 33 Q-B7+ and Black's king cannot escape the checks.

28 N—N5

Although this temporarily removes a piece from the battlefield, it was the only good way for the knight to escape.

28 ...   K—N2

Trying to decide the game with the maneouvre R-R1-R5.

29 N—Q4

Coming to the rescue at the very last moment. Spassky was now in rather bad time-trouble.

29 ...   R—R1?!

Being in time trouble, Black omits the intermediate winning move 29 ... R-Q1! 30 P-B3 (not 30 N-B5+ K-B3!!) and only now 30 ... R-R1!! (30 ... B-Q3 leads nowhere after 31 K-N1!) with the attacking continuation as in the game but leaving White without the square QB3 for his salvation (by the exchange of queens): 31 K-N1 Q-K6+ or 31 N-B3 BxN 32 QxB B-Q3.

30 N—B3   BxN

31 QxB

A must: 31 PxB? R-R5.

31 ...   B—Q3

31 ... R-R5 32 B-B1 B-Q3 gave better chances to fight for a win in the endgame to come.

32 Q—B3!

Again the only move, possibly overlooked by his opponent. 32 K-N1 R-R5 would make White feel miserable.

32 ...   QxQ

33 PxQ   B—K4

Black has the better endgame but his advantage is not decisive because the bishops are of opposite colours. 33 ... BxP 34 R-R1 would lead to simplifications.

34 R—Q7!   K—B3

Preventing 35 BxP.

35 K—N1   BxP

Not 35 ... R-QB1 because of 36 B-K2 with the threat of B-R5.

36 B—K2

White has defended very well and the draw is in sight.

36	...	B—K4
37	K—B1	R—QB1
38	B—R5	R—B2
39	RxR	BxR
40	P—QR4	K—K2
41	K—K2	P—B4
42	K—Q3	B—K4
43	P—B4	K—Q3
44	B—B7	B—N6
45	P—B5+	

Draw agreed.

The first draw in the match and the referee Schmid liked that result best: "It will put both players in the right mood for the match!"

The score 2½:1½ to Spassky.

5

As is well known, when Fischer met Petrosian for the Candidates finals at Buenos Aires, Fischer won the first game but lost the second. This was followed by three draws. Fischer, it was learnt, was suffering from a cold and was taking drugs for it. He was unnaturally quiet the first week. Then he started to complain — about his hotel room, about the food, about playing conditions. His admirers who had been worried cheered up; this meant that Bobby was back on form. He went on to win the next four games in a row — during which period Petrosian, pleading nervous exhaustion, took two days off on his doctor's advice. But this did not affect the final score.

Before the fifth game with Spassky, the rumour spread that Fischer had put fourteen(!) new demands to the Icelandic Chess Federation. He wanted to change rooms. He asked to be allowed to sign bills wherever he went. He wanted more pocket money than his allowance of ten dollars a day, a new Mercedes car (the one he was given was two years old), the option to change the playing room, a larger supply of American newspapers and magazines, personal control of filming (his own off and on switch), a chessboard with squares one eighth of an inch smaller, the use of an indoor tennis court, the exclusive use of the hotel swimming pool, and so on.

The Icelanders kept quiet about these demands and no-one knew to what extent rumours had been exaggerated. Already the hotel swimming pool was closed at 10pm. and Fischer was given the right to use it alone after that time. He felt happy in the swimming pool and sauna bath during the physically exhausting two or three hours spent there from 11pm. on. But, was he back on form was the question that mattered, and the fourth game had raised some doubts.

But the panicky days of Fischer's return plane booking were over. The best sign that everthing was all right was the arrival of the experienced veteran grandmaster Miguel Najdorf from Buenos Aires. He had not wanted to risk the expense of the trip until he felt certain that the match was going to be played to its finish.

By the fifth game the match had become a matter of routine with Spassky arriving on time and Fischer a few minutes late for the game.

Spassky spent much time and energy in the opening and found an ingenious eleventh move. Yet, after Fischer's modest (but wonderfully simple) reply, Spassky found himself fighting against a brick wall. Black's position was unpenetrable and every active move of Spassky's only increased his problems of how to draw. The champion's fruitless efforts were crowned by the worst blunder of his career, at a time when he was again worried by the threat of time-trouble.

Meanwhile, Fischer had been playing with ease, spending relatively little time on his strong moves. How come that the challenger always knew what he was doing? According to Najdorf the secret lay in the nature of Fischer's work in chess. The American grandmaster never bothered too much about the initial moves. He studied the different types of positions, thousands of them, even from the forgotten past, and searched and memorized the reasons for a player's defeat. That way apart from his gift for the game, he possesses an experience and personal knowledge without parallel in chess history. Whatever position arises, with a very few exceptions (e.g. the fourth game), he knows where 'it hurts'. That is how Fischer orientated himself so excellently while Spassky vacillated in the fifth game.

In order to celebrate his victory, Fischer spent more than two hours in the hotel swimming pool the same night. Meanwhile Spassky played tennis with his helper, International Master Nei, at the court near his hotel, until dark at about 11pm. By then he was healthily, physically exhausted and able to forget his oversight and quickly recover for the next game.

White: Spassky
Black: Fischer
Nimzoindian Defence

1	P—Q4	N—KB3
2	P—QB4	P—K3
3	N—QB3	

The first time that Spassky has allowed the Nimzoindian without delay. The reason might be that this way there is a broader choice of lines for White if Fischer again tried the Modern Benoni with 3 ... P-B4.

| 3 | ... | B—N5 |
| 4 | N—B3 | |

Most popular is 4 P-K3, but Spassky likes to keep the option of developing his queen bishop to N5, if possible. With his next move, Fischer prevents it.

4	...	P—B4
5	P—K3	N—B3
6	B—Q3	BxN+
7	PxB	P—Q3

The favourite line of young German Grandmaster Huebner. It could hardly be avoided once White had developed his king knight in the early stage of the game.

| 8 | P—K4 | P—K4 |
| 9 | P—Q5 | |

Spassky reflected too long over each move. Was he surprised by this specific variation? 9 PxBP PxP 10 Q-B2 B-K3! 11 N-Q2 N-QR4 does not allow White to play the intended manoeuvre N-B1-K3-Q5.

| 9 | ... | N—K2 |

The knight is needed for the defence of the king side.

| 10 | N—R4 | |

Considered to be the most active continuation (10 ... N-N3 11 N-B5!), but another question is whether it is actually the best, for in many cases it produces too many simplifications.

| 10 | ... | P—KR3 |

All played before. Black intends 11 ... P-KN4 thereby preventing the advance of White's KB-pawn. Both sides are fighting for more space on the crucial king's wing where the position may become opened.

| 11 | P—B4!? | |

A bolt from the blue. Spassky took much time for this new idea, which revealed the extent of his imagination. It was his bad luck that this attacking move could not do any harm to the opponent. The normal continuation is 11 P-B3 P-KN4 12 N-B5 BxN 13 PxB Q-R4 e.g.

1) 14 B-Q2 0-0-0 15 P-N4 QR-K1 16 K-B2 P-K5! 17 PxP P-KR4 18 PxP RxP 19 Q-B3 R(K1)-R1 20 P-KR3 with equal chances. Donner-Damjanovic, Berlin 1971.

2) 14 Q-B2! 0-0-0 15 P-KR4 P-K5 16 BxKP (16 PxKP is even stronger — Donner) 16 ... NxB 17 PxN QR-K1 18 K-B2 P-B3 19 B-K3 K-N1 20 P-K5!! and White's position was overwhelming. Donner-Damjanovic, Cienfuegos 1972.

11 ....   N—N3!

A great reply by a great player. This modest looking move is by far the best. White's knight is the piece which best adds a dynamic streak to his position, and now it must be removed from the chess board (12 N-B5 BxN 13 PxB NxBP).

Very dangerous would be 11 ... PxP 12 BxP P-KN4 13 P-K5! N-N5 14 P-K6 (not 14 PxP PxB 15 PxN QxP+ 16 Q-K2 N-K6) 14 ... N-KB3 15 B-N3 with a very strong attack as Black rapidly realized.

12 NxN   PxN

Now White no longer has the possibility of pressure along the KB-file. His next move could have waited but without any special reward for doing so.

13 PxP   PxP

The position is blocked and White simply has nothing. Black can easily defend his weak spots while White's are not lesser in number.

14 B—K3?!

White begins to err a little (Black has to play P-N3 anyhow). After 14 0-0 0-0 15 R-N1 P-QN3 16 R-N2 White could hold the balance more easily.

14 ...   P—N3
15 0—0   0—0
16 P—QR4

White strives for action where there is none and creates only a weakness which is not sufficiently compensated by the one arising out of Black's reply.

16 ...   P—QR4!

Played without hesitation, which illustrates Fischer's precise judgement. The completely blocked position does not suit White's pair of bishops and the light-squared one is doomed to passivity throughout the game.

17 R—N1

The best chance to keep Black busy.

17 ...   B—Q2

Doing the same thing to the weak White QR-pawn.

18 R—N2   R—N1

19 R(2)—KB2?

An important decision, removing his pressure from the queen side. But without his heavy pieces White has less opportunity to trouble his opponent.

19 ...   Q—K2

Not 19 ... Q-B2? because of 20 BxRP.

20 B—B2

Defending the QR-pawn and agreeing to the coming simplifications. After 20 P-R3 P-KN4, the move ... P-N5 would be an unpleasant threat.

20 ...   P—KN4

Black has bigger ambitions than just an eventual draw by ... N-N5.

21 B—Q2

Removing the bishop from an exposed square. The slightest deceiving signs of Spassky's (non-existant) initiative have disappeared by now. In the endgame White will have a larger number of weak pawns (all of them on the fourth rank), than Black.

21 ...   Q—K1

Stressing the awkward position of White's pieces which have nothing to do but try to defend his pawns.

22 B—K1

The best counterchance would be to bring the bishop, if possible, to KN3, and attack Black's vital KP.

22	...	Q—N3
23	Q—Q3	

The queen would like to go to KN3, as well.

| 23 | ... | N—R4! |

Sooner or later Black had to exchange rooks and try his chances with the remaining pieces.

24	RxR+	RxR
25	RxR+	KxR
26	B—Q1	

Aiming to bring the queen to QN1.

| 26 | ... | N—B5 |

In case of 26 ... N-B3 (the "strategic move") White would have an excellent chance to activate his pieces with 27 B-KN3!. Now, Black's knight cannot be chased from its stronghold without seriously weakening White's position.

| 27 | Q—B2?? | |

Threatened by a coming time-trouble, and perhaps remembering his omissions in the previous game when in that situation, Spassky loses patience and makes a terrible blunder. White should have tried 27 Q-N1, although he would remain in permanent difficulties (Black's king goes to QB2 and all Black's pieces combine to organize pressure against White's KP).

| 27 | ... | BxP! |

A bolt from the blue from the opposite side. The combination is simple: 28 QxB QxP with the double mating threat (29 K-B2 N-Q6+ etc.); or 28 Q-N1 BxB and 29 ... QxP.

White resigns.

Fischer had evened the score: 2½:2½!

6

After all, it is how one plays chess that really matters. The challenger became more agreeable to discuss the problem of the cameras for some two hours during his spare time. Could the cameraman be taken away so that no living being would stare through the instrument at the players? Impossible! Could the cameras, then, be covered with something black? That did not work either. There was no solution but there was hope. The television crew was ordered to stand by. At the same time, the journalists (some of whom had never heard about chess before and were sent to Reykjavik at short notice because 'chess is big now') were grateful to have another subject to write about. 'The show must go on.' The clouds were very low over Reykjavik and, it seemed, intended never to go away. For weeks, there was a kind of 24-hour twilight on the island and one could not escape the feeling of living in some future distant age when our sun would be dying but life still possible at a reduced intensity.

The wheel of fortune made unbelievable turns in seven days. The Sunday before, it seemed that Fischer was doomed. Who would expect that the challenger would continue the match under those strange and, by then, very unfavourable circumstances (0:2 and one of the losses a forfeit, the first one in the history of the world championship)? Even on the eve of the third game Bobby looked very pale and near to a nervous breakdown.

But his appearance was deceptive. I remember the lost expression on his face before he began, after his eighteen-month absence from competition, to beat Petrosian in the Match of the Century in Belgrade 1970. 'When he starts playing chess, he is another man. He becomes steel!' This was known to Fischer's chess teacher Jack Collins, but not to many others. True, Fischer hesitated to make his first move in the third game. But he made no mistake after that.

Spassky felt no reason to escape an open fight. Najdorf asked excitedly: 'Why did he not play the cautious 4 P-K3 in that game? The champion had prepared hard for eight months and discovered 'serious weaknesses in Fischer's play'. The fourth game gave him more reason to believe this, but he missed his winning opportunities. At the same time Spassky had 'serious weaknesses' too, and it was amazing the way that Fischer knew how to point his finger at them in a different way in every game. For how long can the challenger keep this up?

The sixth game saw the first Queen's Gambit (with Fischer as White) in his chess career. Although Spassky had never lost with Tartakower's line in his many tournament games, this time he could not put up an adequate resistance. Fischer seemed prepared for almost everything. He repeated an improvement from a Soviet competition, and although the loser then was Geller, Spassky's second probably omitted to instruct his player about the dangers of White's fourteenth move. No wonder, for who would have predicted a Queen's Gambit with Fischer on the White side?

White: Fischer
Black: Spassky
Queen's Gambit Declined, Orthodox Defence.

(In order to feel more relaxed, Spassky, for the first time, took a long walk to the tournament hall instead of being driven. As usual Fischer, arriving by car, was several minutes late for the game.)

1   P—QB4!

A surprise! Did the fourth game temporarily shake Fischer's confidence in his traditional 1 P-K4, or was it planned far in advance to search on a larger scale for deficiencies in the champion's opening repertoire.

Fischer has tested this move only once before, in the Interzonal in Palma de Mallorca 1970, and that against Polugaevsky (who, as Black, likes the Sicilian). The game went 1 P-QB4 N-KB3 2 P-KN3 P-B3 3 B-N2 P-Q4. Fischer also opened 1 P-QB4 against Panno in the last round of the same tournament but Panno resigned the game without replying.

1   ...   P—K3

A cautious approach. More ambitious is 1 ... P-K4, as Spassky sometimes used to play, but that would produce a Sicilian with colours reversed and that was not at all Black's idea!

2   N—KB3   P—Q4
3   P—Q4

Another surprise. Fischer never plays the Queen's Gambit as White, and one could rather expect a more reserved Reti system as his second choice. What has Fischer got in mind? Should Black try the Tarrasch Defence, or just the Orthodox? Well, the second choice looked safer, for Spassky had never lost a game with that line.

3   ...   N—KB3
4   N—B3   B—K2
5   B—N5   0—0
6   P—K3   P—KR3
7   B—R4   P—QN3

Tartakower's variation was Spassky's favourite choice in many tournaments. Here he had one more reason for playing it: White developed his KN early and thus is deprived of any dangerous pressure against the Black QP with B-K2-B3 and KN-K2, as

in Portisch-Ivkov, Wijk aan Zee 1972.

Fischer could expect Black's line, but who could expect Fischer to play against it?

8   PxP   NxP

The old 8 ... PxP is playable, but less popular in modern praxis.

9   BxB   QxB
10 NxN

Creating "hanging pawns" in the centre for Black. The alternative is 10 R-B1 B-N2 11 NxN trying to avoid the more active position of Black's bishop on K3, but then Black could answer 11 ... BxN without incurring pawn weaknesses in the centre.

10 ...   PxN
11 R—B1   B—K3

The QN-file may become open later and therefore it is considered preferable not to have the bishop on N2 where it could disturb the activity of Black's heavy pieces.

12 Q—R4   P—QB4
13 Q—R3   R—B1

All known from the books. After 14 B-K2 N-Q2 tournament praxis has shown that White gains nothing.

14 B—N5!

Is this new? Fischer's improvement? No; it was played in the game Furman-Geller, Soviet team competition 1970, but the challenger was quick to notice the value of Furman's idea! The intention is to exchange the bishop for Black's knight and thus expose Black's QB-pawn to a more severe pressure from White's pieces.

14 ...   P—QR3
This is an unwelcome exposure of

Black's QRP, but how else to get rid of the intruder which does not permit Black to complete his development in peace?

15 PxP   PxP

Not 15 ... RxP 16 0-0!

16 0—0   R—R2

Fischer and his conception! Strange, how a recognized line for Black all of a sudden looks not worthy of being played! Black puts his rook on a protected but awkward square and the difficulties remain as to how to develop his knight (in addition to the weak QBP Black's QRP is in need of protection).

Geller suggested 16 ... Q-N2 17 B-K2 (but what if 17 B-R4?) N-Q2.

17 B—K2

The bishop should not be removed too far from the K- side while Black's queen is near it and White's queen busy on the other side. The "loss" of a tempo with the bishop was in fact a gain. Black has a weak QRP and an undeveloped queen side.

17 ...   N—Q2

This allows White's knight to come very effectively into action, but how otherwise is it possible to develop? After 17 ... P-QR4 18 R-B3 (18 R-B2 P-R5 19 B-N5! is probably even better) N-Q2 19 KR-B1 R-K1 20 B-N5 White was clearly better. Furman-Geller, 1970 continued 20 ... B-N5 21 N-Q2 P-Q5 22 PxP PxP 23 QxQ RxQ 24 R-B8+ K-R2 25 N-N3 N-K4 26 R-Q8 R(R)-B2 27 RxR RxR 28 P-B4 B-Q2 29 PxN BxB 30 NxQP R-B8+ 31 K-B2 R-Q8 32 R-Q6 and Black resigned.

18 N—Q4

Producing increased threats to Black's hanging pawns.

18 ...   Q—B1?

Black did not like 18 ... N-B3 19 N-N3 P-B5 (19 ... N-Q2 20 R-B3) 20 QxQ RxQ 21 N-Q4 with an inferior endgame, but the text will make it even more difficult for him in the middlegame.

19 NxB   PxN

20 P—K4!

Striking at the heart of Black's position. After 20 B-N4 Black could defend himself. But after the key move of the game, Black probably could not escape a feeling of being in danger of a sudden and immediate defeat.

20 ...   P—Q5

Being in serious difficulties Black chooses a sharp answer in search for counterchances but it weakens his light squares. Other moves were not much more attractive: 20 ... PxP 21 R-B4 and Black's pawns are all weak and doomed; or 20 ... N-B3 21 P-K5 N-Q2 (21 ... N-K5 22 P-B3) 22 P-B4.

21 P—B4

Controlling the square K5 and threatening B-B4 with greater effect.

21 ...   Q—K2

Black is paying for his loss of time.

22 P—K5!

Fixing the weakness of K6. 22 P-QN4 P-K4 would give Black some counterplay.

22 ...   R—N1

Meeting the immediate threat 23 P-QN4, but everything is hanging by a thread in Black's position. In the case of 22 ... N-N3 (preventing B-B4) 23 Q-QN3! N-Q4 24 P-B5! and the attack would still be strong.

23 B—B4

The bishop becomes an almighty piece, for White has no fear of 23 ... N-N3 having the reply 24 Q-QN3!

23 ...   K—R1

In case of 23 ... N-B1 24 P-B5 Black would have to face the threat P-B6.

24 Q—R3   N—B1

From now on Black is limited to full passivity until the end of the game, but 24 ... RxP 25 BxP was no better. For a long time Black has been positionally lost.

25 P—QN3   P—QR4

26 P—B5

Now is the time to open the KB-file, to penetrate with the heavy pieces around the

opponent's king and at the same time to
have a dangerous passed K-pawn, both for
the middlegame and the endgame.

26	...	PxP
27	RxP	N—R2
28	R(1)—B1	

Bringing the last reserves into the attack.
Not 28 R-B7? N-N4!

| 28 | ... | Q—Q1 |

Black is helpless against the combined
action of all the active White pieces.

| 29 | Q—N3 | |

Preparing mating threats and the centralization of the queen. All White's moves
are simple and very strong.

| 29 | ... | R—K2 |

Trying to cover the second rank. There is
not much else that Black can do. With his
next move White takes away the last useful square of Black's knight, and then he
proceeds with a slow execution.

30	P—KR4	R(1)—N2
31	P—K6	

Directing an eye to Black's B-pawn.
There are now too many threats, among
them 32 Q-K5. Black cannot try 31 ... P-Q6
because of 32 R-Q5.

31	...	R(N2)—B2
32	Q—K5	Q—K1

32 ... P-Q6 33 R(5)-B3 would result in a
hopeless endgame.

| 33 | P—R4! | |

Putting his opponent into a kind of a
zugzwang. Black must wait, as 33 ... N-B3
34 RxN! PxR 35 RxP! leaves his king without shelter.

| 33 | ... | Q—Q1 |

There is nothing else to play: 33 ... K-N1
34 R-B7 loses at once. With his next two
rather neutral moves, White leaves his
opponent with the option to resign.

34	R(1)—B2	Q—K1
35	R(2)—B3	Q—Q1
36	B—Q3	Q—K1
37	Q—K4!	

The same would follow after 36 ... R-B3.
The threat of 38 R-B8+ forces Black to
allow the technical sacrifice of the exchange after which there is no defence
against the mating attack.

37	...	N—B3
38	RxN!	PxR
39	RxP	K—N1
40	B—B4	

The threat is 41 R-B7.

40	...	K—R1
41	Q—B4	

One of several winning moves (41 R-
B7!): 41 ... K-N1 42 QxRP or 42 Q-N3+ K-
R1 43 Q-K5! **Black resigns.**

The challenger took the lead for the first
time: 3½:2½ for Fischer!

7

With thousands of spectators applauding Fischer's classical style win in the sixth game, Spassky did the same, while offering his hand to the challenger. In order not to be touched by his opponent's gracious behaviour, 'I had to go away' said Fischer to friends afterwards. There were, however, no soft feelings in the seventh game, just a cruel fight with the same resoluteness shown on both sides. Spassky was not shaken by his bad start. Just because he played below capacity at the beginning it did not mean that it must be so for the rest of the match. And so, he was ready again for an open struggle, more perhaps than ever before. Fischer was also ready. Ready to try to crush the remnants of the champion's self-confidence. Now seemed to be the most appropriate moment to do so.

In fact, Fischer felt happy that same evening after he took the lead for the first time in the match. There was a casual dinner gathering and Bobby did not think much about the match itself although he needed nothing less than nine more points for victory. He behaved as if the Reykjavik duel was over and mused upon the possibility of keeping the world title for the next thirty years, by which time he would be nearly sixty. Rulers used to dream about a thousand years of their empire, but a chess player could not afford to hope for more than the age at which he would still by physically fit for the task. Anyhow, if his dream comes true it will exceed the record of Dr. Emanuel Lasker who sat on the chess throne for twenty seven years.

With that historical insight Fischer went bowling till five o'clock in the morning. Spassky did not seem to want to comply with his challenger's intentions. In reply to a cautious question as to how the champion felt, a member of Spassky's team said without excitement: 'Nichevo (nothing)! He slept fine!' And that was it.

Was it a symbolic sign when Spassky, before the seventh game, was given an executive chair? It swivels, rolls on castors and rocks gently like Fischer's. Some fan of Fischer's did not like the idea, 'stole' the new chair and moved it away from the stage so that the referee, Schmid, had to look for it and, luckily, brought it back just before the game began. Spassky, sitting for the first time in his armchair, richly upholstered in black leather-like vinyl on a heavy chrome plated steel frame (its list price is 470 dollars and it was sent from New York for the 'advertising value'), copied Fischer's tactics from the previous game and abruptly changed his repertoire with the White pieces. After a twelve year gap Spassky once again opened against Fischer with 1 P-K4.

It was like a glove thrown into his opponent's face. Fischer did not mind and accepted the challenge. He adopted his favourite, double-edged line which Spassky had avoided for so long. White's ninth move showed that Spassky did not want to repeat anything that Bobby had experienced in his tournament praxis. Yet, nothing could surprise Fischer in that position. Spassky's apparently dangerous attack evaporated after a few moves and resulted in an inferior endgame a pawn down.

Spassky was lost again! Fischer knew it and relaxed too early. Playing fast, he missed strong lines several times. After that Spassky held on heroically and made the best move even on move forty, when he was left with only a couple of minutes. The real problem came when he had to seal move forty one. He spent forty five minutes on it and found a miraculous solution which showed that he still had energy and fight. On the next day, after the game, Fischer made a bitter statement about his 'poor play before the adjournment.' He intended never again to repeat it.

White: Spassky
Black: Fischer
Sicilian Defence
  1 P—K4!

This was Spassky's favourite weapon in his match with Petrosian in 1969 when he captured the title, but against Fischer he had not tried it since Mar del Plata 1960! Behind in points for the first time, the champion felt that the moment was ripe to stop avoiding Fischer's pet line.
  1 ...   P—QB4!

Accepting the challenge with the wish to continue his "Blitzkrieg" in the match, having taken 3½ points out of the preceding 4 games.

2	**N—KB3**	**P—Q3**
3	**P—Q4**	**PxP**
4	**NxP**	**N—KB3**
5	**N—QB3**	**P—QR3!**

Najdorf's line, in which Fischer has been the greatest expert in the world since 1958!
  6 B—KN5!

The sharpest line, and over the years the most analyzed one, though without any final conclusion.

6	**...**	**P—K3**
7	**P--B4**	**Q—N3!**

More ambitious than 7 ... B-K2. The game now takes a highly interesting course.
  8 Q—Q2   QxP

The "Poisoned Pawn" variation, Fischer's best weapon. His last win with it was against Parma in Rovinj/Zagreb 1970.
  9 N—N3!

No one tried this seldom played continuation against Fischer. The threat is P-QR3 and R-R2 with the capture of Black's queen. More usual is 9 R-QN1.
  9 ...   Q—R6!

More flexible than the older 9 ... N—B3,

which hoped for a premature 10 P-QR3? N-QR4! Sooner or later Black's queen must be moved into safety. By doing it straight away Black keeps open a bigger choice of plans.
  10 B—Q3

White has the better development in return for the sacrificed pawn, but he will need to open the position in order to be able to make use of it. The alternative was 10 BxN PxB 11 B-Q3 (or B-K2 as in the eleventh game), but White prefers to keep more pieces on the board for the attack which is designed to weaken Black's pawn structure.
  10 ...   B—K2

The advantage of Black's 9th move: he can secure the king side sooner and better.
  11 0—0   P—KR3

Taking the opportunity to get rid of White's unpleasant bishop.

11 ... QN-Q2 would not be new, being known from the games Giterman-Sakharov, USSR Spartakiad 1967, which went 12 QR-K1 P-R3 13 B-R4 Q-N5 (if 13 ... NxP 14 RxN BxB 15 R-R4 Q-N7 16 R-N1) 14 B-B2 with excellent positional com-

pensation for the pawn, and Strekalovsky-Shamkovich, USSR 1968, which continued 12 B-N5!? 0-0 (the Russian analyst Matsukevich suggests instead 12 ... PxB! 13 NxP Q-R5 with an unclear position) 13 BxN(Q7) BxB 14 P-K5 PxP 15 PxP N-Q4 16 NxN PxN 17 R-B3 BxB 18 QxB P-R3 19 Q-Q2 Q-K2 20 R-K1 and White has good compensation for his pawn.

12 B—R4

One of two unclear continuations, but 12 BxN BxB 13 P-K5 PxP 14 N-K4 was less attractive to Spassky at that moment. Therefore White offers another pawn hoping to get more out of it, thanks to the temporarily displaced Black KB.

12	...	NxP
13	NxN	BxB
14	P—B5	

White has no time to count the material. He must open as many files as possible and try to penetrate with his pieces.

14 ...   PxP

15 B—N5+!

The only chance. On 15 Q-B4 B-K2 or 15 Q-B3 0-0 White has nothing. By offering the piece White keeps Black's king in the centre and he can therefore continue to attack.

15 ...   PxB!

The other choice, 15 ... K-K2 16 B-B4, would be unpleasant for Black.

16 NxP+   K—B1

Not 16 ... K-K2? 17 NxP(N5) Q-R3 (otherwise 18 Q-Q6+ would follow) 18 Q-N4+! with a winning attack.

17 NxB   N—B3!

Fischer's wonderful grasp of the game! Black played fast in spite of a very complicated position, and it turns out that White's attack is now evaporating.

18 N—Q6

White decides to fight tamely for a draw. Black's position is more stable than it appears: 18 Q-Q7 P-KN3! 19 QxNP Q-R3 is good for Black.

18 ...   R—Q1

19 NxP(N5)

White may have counted on 19 ... RxQ 20 NxQ R-Q4 21 N-B4 P-KN3 22 QR-Q1 RxR 23 RxR K-K2 24 N-B5 with sufficient counterplay in the endgame. But...

19	...	Q—K2!
20	Q—B4	P—KN3
21	P—QR4	

The attack is over. Black has material and positional advantages (White's knights are displaced). Another win for Fischer?

21 ...   B—N4

A sharp move, but there was nothing wrong with the simple 21 ... K-N2 with an easily won position, and making it more difficult for White to get a rook to the K-file.

| 22 | Q—B4 | B—K6+ |
| 23 | K—R1 | P—B5 |

The activity of White's pieces is now very limited.

24 P—N3

Trying desperately to open files and activate his pieces.

24 ...   P—N4

25 QR—K1   Q—N5

Looking for a superior endgame. Not 25 ... R-Q5? 26 N(5)xR Q-K5+ 27 R-B3.

| 26 | QxQ | NxQ |
| 27 | R—K2 | K—N2 |

27 ... N-B3! could have deprived White of any active continuation. Now Spassky tries his only chance.

28	N—R5	P—N3
29	N—B4	N—Q4
30	N(4)—Q6	B—B4

More efficient was 30 ... K-N3! 31 P-B4 N-B3.

31	N—N7	R—QB1?

Unbelievable! 31 ... N-K6! was still a clear win.

32 P—B4!

An essential attempt to break the chain of black pawns.

32	...	N—K6
33	R—B3	NxP
34	PxP	P—N5
35	R—Q3!	

Having both central files, White keeps the best possibilities for counterplay.

35	...	P—R4
36	P—R3	

Fighting for more air on the K-side.

| 36 | ... | N—R4 |

Forcing the unpleasant White knight to make a decision.

| 37 | N(7)—Q6! | BxN |

In order to free the file for his rook, but White gains a tempo for the journey of his knight to the K-side.

38	NxB	R—B8+
39	K—N2	N—B5

White's knight was too strong.

| 40 | N—K8+! | K—N3 |

See diagram next column.

41 P—R4!!

A problem move. White diminishes the scope of his opponent's king while not prematurely committing his pieces for action. After the obvious 41 R-Q5? P-R4 R-B6! (42 ... R-B7 is not bad either e.g. 43 RxR N-K6+ 44 K-B2 NxR(Q4).) Black would win because White's rook left the third rank too early (Black's threat would be ... N-K6+). White did not spend 45 minutes on his sealed move in vain!

| 41 | .... | P—B3 |

After 41 ... K-B4 42 N-N7+ Black would have to repeat moves (42 ... KxP?? 43 R-Q4 mate). 41 ... R-B1 was an interesting possibility.

42 R—K6!

Everything now is well timed.

| 42 | ... | R—B7+ |

42 ... K-B4 43 N-N7+ offers nothing to Black.

43 K—N1

Not 43 K-N3? R-B1 44 R-Q5 R-B6+! getting to the sixth rank without wasting time.

| 43 | ... | K—B4 |

After 43 ... R-B1 44 R-Q5 White has excellent counterplay: e.g. 44 ... K-B2 45 P-B5 RxN 46 R-Q7+ with a draw. Best was 43 ... RxN! 44 RxR N-Q7!, but after 45 R-K2 N-B6+ 46 K-B2 R-B5 47 RxN PxR 48 KxP RxRP 49 R-QN2 the endgame, although a pawn down, would be an easy draw for White.

44	N—N7+	KxP
45	R—Q4+	K—N6

The last try: 45 ... K-B6 46 R-Q3+ is a draw.

46 N—B5+   K—B6

Hoping a little for 47 R-Q3+ K-B5 gaining a vital tempo by attacking the knight. Not 46 ... K-R6?? 47 R-Q3+ with mate.

47 R(6)—K4!

All these moves were made by White in two minutes. In taking so long over his sealed move he had only left himself 20 minutes for the remaining 15 moves up to the next time control. Neither side can now escape the perpetual check. White also has mating threats on KB4 or K3 if Black moves his rook or knight anywhere.

47 ...   R—B8+
48 K—R2   R—B7+

Black has nothing else: 48 ... P-N6+ 49 NxP brings nothing. Black's pieces do not collaborate as well as those of his opponent.

49 K—N1

Draw agreed.

The second draw in the match. The score: 4:3 in favour of Fischer.

8

Throughout its centuries long history, chess has been the game of a tiny minority of mankind. Now, strange things have happened within a few weeks. This incredible match and the even more incredible Fischer have made the whole world read about chess. 'He is either insane, or very clever, wanting so much more money,' wrote the Washington correspondent of the French newspaper 'Figaro.' At the same time, the Moscow correspondent of the same influential Parisian daily said that 'in the Soviet Union it looked like the struggle between good and evil, where Spassky had the role of Saint George fighting the dragon.'

In the meantime, the show was going on. Fischer addressed another letter to the referee asking in extremely elaborate language that the marble chess board be substituted for a wooden one (the one on which the third game in the backstage room was played). Bobby claimed that the wrong combination of colours on the stone gave the impression that the white squares were bigger than the black ones. Schmid informed Spassky and the champion, having bigger problems with his inferior chess than with this, agreed instantly. The seventh game was played on the wooden board. Spassky saved a half point.

But before the eighth game Fischer asked for the marble board back and blamed the referee for having broken the rules. Schmid was puzzled for Fischer was right. In the rules (Article 18) it states that the same chess equipment, chosen by the players at the beginning of the match, should be used throughout the whole match.

Schmid did not succeed in locating Spassky in time, and the wooden board remained for the eighth game. This time it was of no avail to Spassky. Contrary to the legend, in life 'the dragon' was stronger than the saint'. Spassky, obviously impressed by Fischer's better grasp of the positions in games 5, 6 and 7, played as though he was in a hypnotic trance and took one and a half hours to find a suitable plan after Fischer's not too dangerous novelties on moves 10 and 11. Then, quite unexpectedly, worn out by fatigue and irritated by the approaching time pressure, Spassky made, one after the other, two beginner's blunders and was left the exchange down without any compensation. In a hundred years of The World Chess Championship there was only one other game which resembled this one. That was Fischer's loss by forfeit.

White: Fischer
Black: Spassky
English Opening

1 P—QB4!

Once more! It had given better results in the 6th game, than Fischer's favourite 1 P-K4 in the 4th.

1 ...   P—QB4!

Fischer himself likes to oppose the English in this way, playing in the centre. In the 6th game Spassky played 1 ... P-K3, but had no reason to choose it now.

2 N—QB3   N—QB3
3 N—B3   N—B3

It took rather a long time for Black to decide on this move. The alternatives were 3 ... P-K3 or 3 ... P-KN3.

4	P—KN3	P—KN3
5	B—N2	B—N2
6	0—0	0—0
7	P—Q4	PxP

Putting his hopes in the activity of his minor pieces in return for the spatial advantage now delivered to White. More to the classical taste would be 7 ... P-Q3 which would transpose into the Yugoslav variation of the King's Indian Defence, in which Black tries to have better strongholds in the centre.

8 NxP   NxN

The sacrifice of the pawn with 8 ... P-Q3 9 NxN PxN 10 BxP would be unsound, and 8 ... N-KN5 or 8 ... Q-N3 9 N-B2 (or 9 N-N3) would be of doubtful value for Black.

9 QxN   P—Q3

This is the line which Spassky's second Geller used to play himself in various competitions.

10 B—N5!

Although the closed systems have never been the speciality of Fischer before this match, now he demonstrates his ability to produce novelties anywhere! Whether the move was the best or not it produced a psychological shock in his opponent who had already begun to respect Fischer's excellent judgement from previous games (11 ... N-N3! in game 5, and 14 B-N5! in game 6).

The idea is reminiscent of the strategy from the game Hort-Unzicker, Venice 1969, which went 10 Q-Q3 N-Q2 11 Q-B2 N-B4 12 B-N5! P-KR3 13 B-K3 B-B4 14 Q-Q2 K-R2 15 B-Q4 BxB 16 QxB with better play for White.

The move 10 Q-Q3 has given good results several times (but now it would not be a novelty!). For instance, 10 Q-Q3 P-QR3 (or 10 ... N-Q2 11 P-N3! N-B4 12 Q-Q2 B-Q2 13 B-N2 P-QR4 14 N-Q5 BxB 15 QxB B-B3 16 QR-Q1 BxN 17 RxB Q-N3 18 R-N1! KR-B1 19 P-KR4 Q-Q1 20 P-K4! with strong pressure, Gufeld-Damjanovic, Skopje 1971) 11 B-K3 B-B4 (or 11 ... N-N5, 12 B-Q4 N-K4 13 Q-Q1 with the better game, Furman-Stein, USSR 1971) 12 Q-Q2 Q-Q2 13 B-Q4! QR-B1 14 BxN! PxB 15

N-Q5 with advantage to White, Smejkal-Stein, Tallin 1971.

The idea of the move in the game is to provoke Black's weakening ... P-KR3 and then to apply a strategy similar to that in the above mentioned games.

Not 10 Q-R4 Q-R4 with excellent counterplay for Black on the Q-side.

10 ...   B—K3

Black does not accept the invitation to 10 ... P-KR3 11 B-Q2 and 12 Q-Q3 as was played in many tournament games. The threat is 11 ... N-Q4.

11 Q—B4!

Another unusual move and a surprise! The shock was now complete and Spassky took about an hour to find a suitable plan! White has removed his queen from an exposed square, preventing ... P-KR3. Now White may exercise pressure on the KN5-Q8 diagonal and along the Q-file with his rook because his queen has found another, active square.

11 ...   Q—R4

A known idea to build up the pressure on the Q-side and counterbalance White's advantage in space. After 11 ... Q-Q2 12 KR-Q1 QR-B1 13 P-N3 White's pressure along the Q-file would be unpleasant; but 11 ... N-Q2 threatening 12 ... P-B3, was quite playable.

12 QR—B1

Defending the knight and preparing to protect the QB-pawn with P-N3. Black still has to think about his QN-pawn, which for a while was taboo (12 BxP? QR-N1 and 13 ... RxP).

12 ...   QR—N1

Defending the pawn and preparing for counter-action with ... P-QR3 and ... P-QN4.

13 P—N3

By now Fischer had spent half an hour, Spassky one and a half hours.

13 ...   KR—B1

Black was left with a little less than an hour for the remaining 27 moves up to the time control, but if nothing else he has solved the problem of how to develop.

14 Q—Q2

Another unexpected change of attitude. Although incurring some loss in time, White can afford it in order to strengthen his position in the centre. Perhaps Black was puzzled that he could not obtain some advantage from it.

14 ...   P—QR3

15 B—K3

Turning his attention to the Q-side and preparing the centralization of his QB to Q4. At the same time there is a threat in B-R7.

15 ...   P—QN4?

Tiredness and the simple oversight of the loss of the exchange, perhaps caused by the influence of White's slow manoeuvring. Sound was 15 ... R-B2 16 KR-Q1 R(1)-QB1 with an even game.

16 B—R7   PxP?

Black is absent-minded and plays quickly. A better chance was 16 ... R-R1 17 BxR RxB 18 B-Q4 PxP with some control of the central squares and the possibility of advancing his pawns.

17 BxR   RxB

18	PxP	BxP
19	KR—Q1	N—Q2??

Once more, and what a blunder! Influenced by his mistake on the 15th move Black is blinded and does not see something which in his normal state of mind he would be able to notice in a game of lightning chess. Normal was 19 ... K-B1 with hopes to fight for a draw.

20	N—Q5	QxQ
21	NxP+	

Of course! Black is lost, an exchange down and without any compensation for it.

21	...	K—B1
22	RxQ	KxN
23	RxB	R—N8+
24	B—B1	N—B4
25	K—N2	P—QR4

Trying his only chance to capture the white QR-pawn.

26 P—K4

Aimed at undermining the position of Black's knight. Also, 26 P-K3 P-R5 27 B-Q3 R-QR8 28 B-K4 P-R6 29 B-Q5 was good enough.

26 ...   B—R8

Trying to stop P-K5 by ... P-B3, but his position is hopeless anyhow.

27	P—B4	P—B3
28	R—K2	K—K3

Meeting the threat of P-K5.

29 R(2)—QB2   B—N7

Preventing R-B1.

30	B—K2	P—R4?
31	R—Q2	B—R6
32	P—B5+	PxP
33	PxP+	K—K4
34	R(4)—Q4	KxP

35	R—Q5+	K—K3
36	RxQP+	K—K2
37	R—QB6	

Black resigns.

The score: the challenger increased his lead to 5:3!

9

Jerry Weintraub (former promoter of Elvis Presley) and Sid Bernstein (one time manager of the Beatles) were in town. The little known personality of Robert Fischer had waved a magic wand, attracting the distinguished presence of people from the more lucrative world of pop music. Weintraub admitted, and he certainly knows what he is talking about, that in his career he had never witnessed a faster rise into the sky of a new star. In a matter of weeks Bobby Fischer had become a 'super-star,' the man of the year.

Having a different approach to the problem of a chess star, Weintraub checked the reactions in the tournament hall and found out that the tall, good-looking Fischer had a definite appeal to girls. Alas, Bobby concluded long ago that 'chess is much more interesting.' At the same time Fischer's lawyer, Paul Marshall, predicted that a month after the match Robert Fischer would be a true American millionaire, the first one in the annals of chess! Many grandmasters in the past had lived in poverty, but Fischer's merits were enormous.

'What is new?' That was the way to say 'good-morning' among the reporters in Reykjavik. Well 'the agreement has finally been reached' and the ABC cameras were in the hall for the eighth game, but Fischer 'did not know about that' when he was playing and afterwards he threatened to walk out. An urgent meeting was called. Spassky had no say in the matter and meanwhile had to be content with the same luxury chair as was used by Fischer.

Is the real fight over? After the forfeit Spassky had made only two draws out of six games! The champion was in a deep crisis and his only psychological chance now was that having reached the bottom he could only get better.

The eighth game was the worst one of the match, almost a disaster for the title holder. It is not that Fischer played that game so well. On the contrary, it was his least impressive performance. But after having experienced Fischer's excellent judgement in the fifth, sixth and seventh games, it seemed that Spassky felt paralyzed at any novelty introduced by the challenger. Was this disability that was preventing his playing like a champion, to last, or was it just an episode?

Before having to find out the answer for himself, Spassky postponed the ninth game, scheduled for Sunday, July 30th. Although a member of his entourage had said the preceeding evening that Spassky wanted to play (so as not to repeat the complaints of 'high blood pressure' or 'nervous exhaustion' made by Larsen and Petrosian, Fischer's opponents in the qualification matches), the doctor discovered on Sunday morning that Spassky had a cold in the head and a sore throat.

'How about that?' was the short comment of an American radio station. Fred Cramer, an official of the United States Chess Federation, asked to be shown the doctor's certificate, adding perhaps a little bit to the psychological torture for the depressed champion. Grandmaster Lombardy explained that it was Fischer's wish to point at the weakness of the rule that a player may postpone only three times in a case of illness. 'It would be much better to give the right of postponement for whenever a player does not feel fit,' said Fischer's second. He talked sense.

Another two days of rest could only be welcome if it was to bring the match back onto its natural course. In the meantime, there were false rumours that Spassky's second, Geller, had flown to Moscow at short notice in order 'to report about the critical situation in the match', and two days later Icelandic Radio announced incorrectly that Spassky's wife Larissa was coming to Reykjavik.

The panicky news was an exaggeration. Spassky played and lost his regular tennis game 6-3, 6-1, 6-1. Like his Estonian compatriot Paul Keres, Spassky's opponent Nei is an experienced tennis player and Spassky was pleased with this score: 'It could have been worse.'

In the ninth game everything went according to the established routine. Spassky was on stage in time, Fischer almost ten minutes late. An American chess friend explained that it could not only be a psychological weapon but also Bobby's reluctance to face the 'embarassing' situation of sitting there and having nothing to do before the clock was started. This time Spassky could not sit in his chair long. After each of his moves he stood up and walked away.

Another of Fischer's novelties came on the ninth move but his novelties, by now, were also part of the routine. This time Spassky was not shaken. The game itself was rather uneventful although Fischer's new idea in the opening might have a lasting importance for Spassky's favourite line. For the sake of prestige the draw was agreed several moves later than necessary. Fischer behaved nicely, and was the first to whisper the expected word.

White: Spassky
Black: Fischer
Semi-Tarrasch Defence
1   P—Q4

Back to the planned strategy of before the match! The first, third and fifth games were also opened by the title holder in this way. But is the "poisoned pawn" line going to be discussed again?

1   ...   N—KB3
2   P—QB4   P—K3

Fischer's approach in this match is cautious. Will he never play 2 ... P-KN3?

3   N—KB3

As in the first and the third games.

3   ...   P—Q4

Sharper is 3 ... P-B4 (3rd game), but now there is no need for it.

4   N—B3   P—B4!

Something different! In the first game Black played 4 ... B-N5. The move here is also a kind of a challenge, for Spassky is an expert on any form of the Tarrasch Defence, playing White or Black.

5   BPxP!   NxP
6   P—K4!

Starting with this move Spassky developed a new strategy for White and had an excellent victory against Petrosian in 1969. What has Fischer up his sleeve when deliberately entering this dangerous variation?

A good alternative is 6 P-K3, but it became less popular when Spassky showed a way to make good use of the full pawn centre.

6   ...   NxN
7   PxN   PxP
8   PxP   N—B3!

Everyone played 8 ... B-N5 here and had a bad time of it in recent years. Yet, the move in this game is not quite new and was played in the game Platonov-Krogius (another member of Spassky's team in Reykjavik) in Leningrad in 1971, but there

it only resulted in a different order of
moves.

After 8 ... B-N5+ 9 B-Q2 BxB+ (9 ... Q-R4
10 R-QN1!) 10 QxB 0-0 11 B-B4 N-Q2 12 0-
0 P-QN3 13 QR-Q1 B-N2 14 K R-K1 R-B1
15 B-N3 N-B3 16 P-Q5! PxP 17 PxP R-B4
18 P-Q6 B-Q4 19 Q-B4 N-R4 20 Q-Q4 N-
B3 21 Q-KB4 N-R4 22 Q-Q4 N-B3 23 R-
K5! BxN 24 PxB RxR 25 QxR R-K1 26 Q-
B4 R-B1 27 B-R4 Q-N1 28 Q-K5 R-Q1 29
Q-K7 White was very much better.
Olafsson-Unzicker, Lugano 1970.

9   B—QB4

The most active square for the bishop,
from where it supports the break P-Q5.

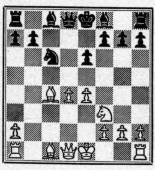

9   ...   P—QN4!

This is Fischer's new idea! Black chases
White's bishop from the strong diagonal
and gains time and space for the active
development of his pieces on the queen
side.

After 9 ... B-N5+ 10 B-Q2 BxB+ (or 10 ...
Q-R4 11 P-Q5! BxB+ 12 QxB QxQ+ 13
KxQ N-R4 14 QR-QB1! K-K2 15 K-K3 R-
Q1 16 K R-Q1 P-B3 17 B-N5 with superior
ending for White, Platonov-Krogius,
Leningrad 1971) 11 QxB 0-0 12 0-0 P-QN3
(12 ... Q-R4?! 13 Q-K2 Q-R4 14 QR-N1 P-
QN3 15 KR-B1 B-N2 16 B-R6!, Hort-
Platonov, Wijk aan Zee 1970) 13 QR-Q1!
(this is the right way to develop the rooks
because White's chances lie on the king
side) B-N2 14 K R-K1! R-B1 (or 14 ... N-R4
15 B-Q3 R-B1 16 P-Q5! PxP 17 P-K5 N-B5
18 Q-B4 N-N7 19 BxP+! KxB 20 N-N5+ K-
N3 21 P-KR4! R-B5 22 P-R5+ K-R3 23
NxP+ K-R2 24 Q-B5+ K-N1 25 P-K6! with
a strong attack. Polugaevsky-Tal, Moscow
1970) 15 P-Q5 PxP 16 BxP N-R4 17 Q-B4

Q-B2 18 Q-B5 BxB 19 PxB White has the
advantage. Spassky-Petrosian, fifth match
game 1969.

10   B—Q3

Not 10 BxNP? Q-R4+. On 10 B-N3 the
bishop would be exposed to Black's ... N-
R4, but 10 B-K2 was a serious alternative in
order to give better support to an eventual
P-Q5.

10   ...   B—N5+

Now is the right moment for this move.
Black should reduce the number of pieces
on the board while White has a full pawn
centre.

11   B—Q2   BxB+
12   QxB   P—QR3
13   P—QR4!?

Trying to dissolve Black's queen side,
but it loses a move and slows down White's
development. Nevertheless, it is difficult to
exploit the weakness on QB5 because of
Black's ... Q-N3 and his pressure on the un-
stable Q-pawn.

13   ...   0—0!

Ready to meet 14 PxP with 14 ... NxP!

14   Q—B3   B—N2

Black is not afraid of 15 PxP PxP 16
RxR QxR 17 BxP N-R2!, or 16 BxP RxR+
17 QxR Q-N3 with too much initiative for a
(temporarily) sacrificed pawn.

15   PxP   PxP
16   0—0   Q—N3!?

A drawish outcome now looks inevitable, but this move is an inaccuracy which
was left unpunished. Necessary first was 16
... RxR! 17 RxR and then 17 ... Q-N3 so
that 18 P-Q5 P-N5 19 R-N1 PxP 20 PxP
PxQ 21 RxQ N-Q1 22 P-Q6 would not

work because of 22 ... BxN 23 PxB N-K3.

Not 16 ... P-N5 17 Q-B5 when White's queen has a dominating position.

17 QR—N1! P—N5

18 Q—Q2

More chances would be given by 18 P-Q5 PxP 19 PxP PxQ (if 19 ... Q-Q1 20 Q-B2! QxP 21 BxP+ K-R1 22 B-K4 and Black is having difficulties) 20 RxQ N-Q1 21 B-B4! (this move would not be possible if rooks had been exchanged on the 16th move because of 21 ... P-B7).

18 ... NxP

Of course! Otherwise, White would have a threat in P-Q5.

19 NxN QxN

20 RxP Q—Q2

20 ... R-R7 was also quite good: 21 QxR QxR 22 R-N1 Q-Q5.

21 Q—K3 KR—Q1

21 ... R-R6 would be met by 22 R-Q4.

22 KR—N1

The simplest, freeing the safe square for an eventual retreat of the bishop.

22 ... QxB

Not 22 ... BxP?? 23 BxB Q-Q8+ 24 Q-K1.

23	QxQ	RxQ
24	RxB	P—N4
25	R—N8+	RxR
26	RxR+	K—N2
27	P—B3	R—Q7
28	P—R4	P—R3
29	PxP	PxP

Draw agreed.

The score: 5½:3½ in favour of Fischer.

10

After almost endless bad weather, the sun began to shine on the 2nd of August. It was the worst July in Iceland for 17 years. It was the worst July for Spassky, too.

Bobby's willingness to discuss the possibility of removing the cameramen or covering the cameras with something black, was misinterpreted as a sign that the challenger would change his attitude as soon as things improved for him in the match. Fischer was furious when he heard that the eighth game had been filmed. His lawyer who signed the agreement flew home, and so did the television crew, for the American Broadcasting Company saw no more hope.

People close to Bobby began to wonder whether he really cared for money that much, although he speaks so much about it. There was even an impression that Fischer had no real concept what 10,000 or 100,000 dollars really meant. He played with sums as with toys, and it was his chess and social prestige that he really cared for.

The lack of filming deprived the organizers of perhaps 100,000 dollars income. Fischer was not bothered by that, nor by his, or Spassky's, financial loss. Spassky kept out of it, having bigger personal worries. Things were not tragic for the Icelandic Chess Federation, as the government declared itself ready to cover the deficit in the match budget. A 'fishing war' was being prepared for the autumn, when Iceland would proclaim an extension of her territorial waters to 50 miles, and it could not be bad to have, thanks to the match, so much advance publicity for the country.

With the TV cameras definitely out, Fischer had no more reason to excite himself and others, and the only remaining problem was to give him, apart from milk and orange juice, a sufficient supply of drinking water (he eats salty herrings during play). The water is excellent, as in other countries a few hundred years ago. Iceland is an isolated spot, not yet spoilt by pollution, and there is a big business prospect of exporting good natural drinking water to less lucky industrial states. Such is civilization.

Spassky looked fine, but his feeble voice disclosed his nervous exhustion. On the first sunny free day he took a long walk and sat on a rock on the sea shore, reflecting in solitude how to pull himself back into the match. For the moment he felt he had no energy for another risky attempt. So he decided to make a cautious approach, to keep the 'status quo' until he could recapture his will to fight fiercely.

It was to no avail. The tenth game was the first one in the match where both players employed a line which they could both predict before the match, and had prepared for accordingly. Spassky's general belief in the soundness of the Breyer variation, shared by many Soviet grandmasters, was met by Fischer's thorough analysis of the possibilities in that kind of position. Once more, Black had problems to solve and another time scramble occurred. Spassky made some small slips and Fischer's impeccable play did the rest.

White: Fischer
Black: Spassky
Ruy Lopez
   1 P—K4!

The psychological surprises were over. So, back to normal and to the favourite move!

   1 ...   P—K4!

No Sicilian this time! Spassky needed time to recover and did not wish to risk a further deterioration of his position in the match.

2	N—KB3	N—QB3
3	B—N5	P—QR3
4	B—R4	N—B3
5	0—0	B—K2
6	R—K1	P—QN4
7	B—N3	P—Q3

At Santa Monica 1966, Spassky played the Marshall against Fischer with 7...0-0 8 P-B3 P-Q4!?, but times are different now, and that risky line has been analyzed more thoroughly in the meantime.

8	P—B3	0—0
9	P—KR3	

At last, here was a position which had been expected before the start of the match.

   9 ...   N—N1

The Breyer line, one of Spassky's favourites. Black connects better the exposed pawns on the Q-side and prepares a more flexible placement of his minor pieces.

10	P—Q4	QN—Q2
11	QN—Q2	

Fischer used to play 11 N-R4, so this would have been no surprise to his opponent. His game with Barczay at Sousse 1967 had the continuation 11 N-R4 PxP 12 PxP N-N3 13 N-KB3! with advantage in the centre, but there are other possibilities for Black like 11 N-R4 R-K1 12 N-B5 B-B1 or 11 N-R4 N-N3 12 N-Q2 P-B4 13 PxBP PxP 14 N-B5 BxN 15 PxB, Fischer-Benko, U.S. Championshop 1965.

The sharp line is 11 P-B4 P-B3 12 P-B5 Q-B2 13 BPxP BxP 14 B-N5 PxP 15 BxN PxB 16 QxP N-K4 17 QN-Q2 R-Q1 18 Q-K3 N-Q6 19 Q-R6 B-B5! 20 QxBP R-Q3 21 Q-B3 NxR 22 RxN Q-Q1 23 R-K2 with chances for both sides, Fischer-Portisch, Second Piatigorsky Cup, Santa Monica 1966.

11	... **B—N2**
12	**B—B2**

This gives better cover to the KP and prepares an annexation of space on the Q-side by pawn advances.

  12 ...   R—K1

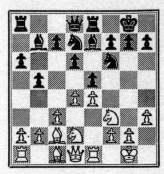

  13 P—QN4

Spassky against Unzicker, Santa Monica 1966, had little with 13 N-B1 B-KB1 14 N-N3 P-N3 15 B-N5 P-R3 16 B-Q2 B-N2.

The move in the game aims to prevent Black's P-QB4, and thus emphasize a strategical weakness of Breyer's line, which postpones that manoeuvre for too long. But, in comparison with the game Fischer-Stein, Sousse 1967, which went 9 P-KR3 B-N2 10 P-Q4 N-QR4 11 B-B2 N-B5 12 P-QN3 N-N3 13 QN-Q2 N(N3)-Q2 14 P-QN4!, it is Black who is a move ahead here.

  13 ...   B—KB1

The necessary reply. 13...P-QR4, 13...PxP and 13...P-Q4 look less solid: a) 13...P-QR4 14 N-N3 R PxP 15 BPxP R-N1 16 N-R5 P-B3, Suetin-Tringov, Titovo-Uzice 1966, and now 17 NxB RxN 18 B-N3 would have given White the better game; b) 13...PxP 14 PxP P-QR4 15 PxP P-B4 16 B-N2 QxP 17 P-QR4 P-N5 18 N-B4 Q-B2 19 P-K5 QPxP 20 PxKP N-Q4 21 KN-Q2 N(Q2)-N3, Ciric-Robatsch, Beverwijk 1967, and now 22 P-K6! gives a clear advantage to White.

  14 P—QR4

Parma against Unzicker, Berlin 1971, tried a different plan: 14 B-N2 N-N3 15 P-R3, threatening P-QB4. A similar idea was also played in Ciric-Kuijpers, Beverwijk

1967: 14 B-N2 P-N3 15 P-R3 B-N2 16 P-Q5 N-N3 17 P-B4 PxP 18 P-QR4 P-B3 19 PxP BxP 20 P-R5 N-B1 21 NxBP with the better game.

14 ...   N—N3

This looks very solid. Black invites his opponent to say what he wants to do on the Q-side. In the game Balashov-Podgaets, Moscow 1966, the unclear continuation 14 ... P-B4 15 NPxP KPxP (or 15 ... QPxP 16 PxKP QNxP 17 NxN RxN 18 P-KB4 with advantage) 16 P(B3)xP QPxP was played. But interesting is 14 ... P-QR4! 15 RPxP RPxP 16 B-N2 NPxP 17 BxP P-B3 draw, Kavalek-Portisch, Wijk aan Zee 1969.

15 P—R5

15 PxP PxP offers nothing to White. In this position the game Minic-Petrosian, Rovinj-Zagreb 1970, was agreed drawn!

15 ...   N(N3)-Q2

Establishing the previous situation for Black without having committed himself with any pawn weakness.

16 B—N2

The only good developing move at White's disposal. After 16 P-Q5 P-B3 17 P-B4 NPxP 18 PxP BxP 19 NxBP Q-B2 Black would have very good counterplay.

16 ...   Q—N1

Black has a solid position, but it is difficult to find an appropriate plan. With the move in the game Black gives additional protection to his KP (along the diagonal QN1-K4, and is again ready for 17 P-Q5? P-B3 18 P-B4 NPxP 19 PxP BxP 20 NxBP QxP), but the queen manoeuvre is somehow artificial.

17   R—N1!

All of a sudden Black has difficulties. What is he to do against the positional threat 18 P-B4? White's last move protects his QB and QNP and builds pressure along the QN-file after P-QB4.

17 ...   P—B4

17...Q-R2 18 P-B4! KPxP 19 BxP would not work out well for Black. Therefore, he tries his only chance for active play.

18 NPxP   QPxP

18...KPxP 19. P(B3)xP PxP 20 P-K5 opens diagonals towards the black king.

19 PxKP   N(Q2)xP

20 NxN   QxN

21 P—QB4   Q—B5

Black tries his best chance—the threat along the Q-file.

22 BxN

Aiming to win a pawn or have some positional advantage on the Q-side. It is also necessary to diminish his opponent's pressure along the central files.

22 ...   QxB

22...PxB 23 PxP QR-Q1 24 R-K3 would be favourable for White.

23 PxP

With the possibility of using the square QB4 for the knight.

23 ...   KR—Q1

Why not the other rook? Well, 23...QR-Q1 24 Q-B1 Q-QB6 25 B-R4! would put Black in difficulties because the rook on K1 would be left hanging.

24 Q—B1

Removing the queen from the unpleasant pin. Not 24 P-K5? Q-N4 winning.

24 ...   Q—QB6

25 N—B3

Marshalling pieces towards Black's under-protected K-side.

25 ... QxP?

Unclear was 25...P-B5 26 PxP BxRP 27 P-K5. But instead of the move in the game, which leaves the K-side unprotected, a better chance was 25...PxP 26 RxP B-R3.

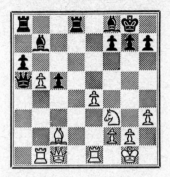

26 B—N3!

After 26 PxP Black could defend. With the move in the game White saves a tempo for the attack and Black is, all of a sudden, in a critical situation.

26 ... PxP
27 Q—KB4 R—Q2

The only defence. After 27...P-B5 28 BxP PxB 29 RxB Q-R4 30 P-N4! QxRP 31 N-N5 Black would soon be lost.

28 N—K5 Q—B2
29 QR—Q1! R—K2

Not 29 ... RxR? 30 BxP+ K-R1 31 N-N6+ PxN 32 Q-R4 mate. The alternative was 29 ... QR-Q1 30 BxP+ RxB 31 QxR+ QxQ 32 NxQ RxR 33 RxR BxP 34 N-N5 with good winning chances for White. Now, White has the Q-file for his combination, which will result in the gain of material.

30 BxP+ RxB
31 QxR+ QxQ
32 NxQ BxP

Better than 32 ... KxN 33 R-Q7+ which leaves Black without any material compensation for the lost exchange.

33 RxB

33 N-R6+ would lose a precious tempo in blocking Black's passed pawns: 33 ... PxN 34 RxB P-B5!

33 ... KxN

34 R—Q7+ K—B3
35 R—N7

The best way to stop the pawns and keep active rooks.

35 ... R—R8+?

In time pressure, Black misses the better chance 35...P-N5 36 K-B1 R-B1! 37 R-QB4 R-K1! (not 37...K-K3 38 R(7)xQNP) and White would be faced with difficulties in bringing his material advantage to effect.

36 K—R2 B—Q3+
37 P—N3 P—N5
38 K—N2 P—R4

38...B-K4 might have been better, but after 39 P-B4 B-Q5 40 P-N4 it would still be difficult for Black.

39 R—N6 R—Q8
40 K—B3?

40 P-B4 was the right move.

40 ... K—B2?

Again, 40 ... P-N4! would make the mass of white pawns less dangerous and would thus increase the chances of a draw. Now the adjourned position is hopeless for Black.

41	K—K2	R—Q4
42	P—B4	

Of course! It prevents B-K4 and activates the pawn majority on the K-side.

43	P—N4	P—N3
43	P—N4	PxP
44	PxP	

The threat is to build up a kind of a zugzwang with 44...K-B3 45 R-R6 K-B2 46 P-N5 and later the pin by R-Q7. Therefore, Black fights desperately with his next move for more space and more mobility for his bishop.

44	...	P—N4

Black's best chance to get strongholds for his bishop and some counterplay, instead of being slowly strangled.

45	P—B5	

After 45 PxP B-K4! Black could feel easier because White's pawns would be less secure.

45	...	B—K4
46	R—N5!	K—B3

Black has no good alternative.

47	R(4)xP	B—Q5

Looking desperately for another chance; 47...PxR 48 RxR P-N6 49 RxB! KxR 50 K-Q3 would win easily in the pawn endgame.

48	R—N6+	K—K4
49	K—B3	

Threatening mate with the rook on K6 and preventing Black's K-B5.

49	...	R—Q1
50	R—N8	

Not letting the Black rook take the KR-file.

50	...	R—Q2

50...PxR 51 RxR P-N6 52 R-QN8 P-N7 53 R-N5+ and 54 K-K4 wins easily.

51	R(4)—N7	R—Q3
52	R—N6	R—Q2
53	R—N6	

Decisive.

53	...	K—Q4
54	RxP	B—K4
55	P—B6	K—Q5
56	R—N1	

Black resigns (56 ... BxP 57 R-Q1+).
Fischer leads 6½:3½.

11

So it seemed that the end of the great Soviet chess empire was taking on the appearance of a strangely quiet, easy, and uneventful death. An Argentinian radio reporter was informed from Moscow about 'the sorrow of millions of Soviet chess fans and the diminished home prestige of the champion.' Outwardly, Spassky looked abandoned to his fate while watching the evening bridge game in the lobby of his hotel. Journalists were still chasing the whereabouts of, and human stories about, the two big competitors, and, while complaining that there was no sports event in their experience so shrouded in secrecy and mystery, contemplated on which day of August they would be able to return home and enjoy a little the remnants of summer in the South.

The sky over Reykjavik was rather clear now, and so looked the outcome of the match, although officially it was not half over. Yet, on Sunday, at five dollars entry fee, the tournament hall was packed by thousands of spectators. The act of execution is highly attractive, and there is always the unknown.

Spassky's first move had a slightly electrifying effect. It was the king pawn, the move which he had avoided against Fischer for twelve years, not wanting to go through the hell of Fischer's thoroughly analyzed sharp lines. But now the hell was elsewhere too. Whatever the move meant, it did not indicate a lack of fighting spirit.

True, Spassky also opened that way in the seventh game. But that was at the moment when he had to make a desperate attempt in order to equalize the score in the match. Then he was lost, and he returned to his queen pawn in the ninth game. Now the king pawn was not the same, for Spassky had to know what he was entering this time. More than by the score, the title holder was under the pressure of his creative impotence in almost all the preceding games. He had to do something in order to justify his chess career.

Naturally enough, the line used in the seventh game, but less frequently played in tournaments, was repeated. Spassky had nothing to hope for elsewhere. For Fischer, it was also his second game with that specific continuation. On the tenth move Spassky varied, but after thirteen moves the position was still of a known type.

Then Spassky took thirty minutes to decide what to do next. It is hard to guess whether his next move was prepared or not. Spassky said it was not. Probably it was not prepared for White would not have waited — but would have played the same variation in the seventh or ninth game rather than wait until now.

White's paradoxical manoeuvre, the fruit of sudden inspiration, encircled again the daring black queen and threatened her capture. Fischer could not put up a proper resistance and was, surprisingly quickly, lost. There was something dramatic in Spassky's achievement, just at the point when an eventual loss of the match threatened to be transformed into a most severe defeat which would be a personal tragedy, for a very pleasant man. Spassky was not on the stage when Fischer stopped the clock and waited in vain to shake hands, before leaving. When Spassky appeared alone between the curtains and stepped on to the stage in order to sign the score sheets, he continually gave signs with his hands, trying to quieten the roaring applause.

White: Spassky
Black: Fischer
Sicilian Defence

1   P—K4!

This reflects the fighting mood of the champion who is at a disadvantage in points!

1   ...   P—QB4!

Accepting the challenge, as in the 7th game, with the wish to crush, as rapidly as possible, the remaining hopes of the losing man in the duel.

2	N—KB3	P—Q3
3	P—Q4	PxP
4	NxP	N—KB3
5	N—QB3	P—QR3
6	B—KN5!	

Entering the same variation as in the 7th game.

6	...	P—K3
7	P—B4	Q—N3!

Black is also ready for that type of a fight.

8	Q—Q2	QxP
9	N—N3	

It is natural that Spassky looks for his chance to this rare continuation, where Fischer has less experience from his abundant praxis with the Najdorf variation.

9   ...   Q—R6

Fischer's improvement, which leaves Black a more flexible choice of plans. Black's queen seems to be safe now...

10   BxN!

White missed this chance of weakening Black's pawn structure in the 7th game, but faced an unpleasant dilemma after 10 B-Q3 B-K2 11 0-0 P-R3! Nevertheless, the move in the game has been played before.

10   ...   PxB

11   B—K2!

This is different, too, from the seventh game. White keeps the Q-file open to put pressure on Black's QP, and forces Black to waste a move to prevent 12 B-R5.

11   ...   P—KR4

This is new. 11 ... N-B3 was known to be good for White: 12 0-0 and now: a) 12 ... B-Q2 13 K-R1 B-K2 14 B-R5 R-KB1 15 Q-K3 N-R4 16 P-B5 NxN 17 BPxN! 0-0-0 18 N-Q5 PxN 19 PxP B-N4 (19 ... QR-K1 20 Q-R7!) 20 KR-B1+ K-N1 21 QxB and White is clearly better, Angantysson-Ogaard, Denmark 1968; b) 12 ... B-N2 13 R-B3 B-Q2 (13 ... 0-0?! 14 P-B5 P-R3 15 QR-KB1 K-R2 16 R-R3 gives White a decisive attack, Balashov-Schaufelberger, Vilnius 1967) 14 P-B5 R-QB1 15 R-N3! R-KN1 16 R-KB1 with a clear advantage, Minic-Buljovcic, Yugoslavia 1966.

12   0—0   N—B3

12 ... Q-N5 13 Q-K3 N-Q2 was an interesting possibility to allow the queen to escape.

13   K—R1

This prophylaxis is a waste of time at this moment. The right continuation is 13 N-N1! at once.

13   ...   B—Q2?

Black prepares to put his king into safety on the Q-side, and is not aware of the dangers. Correct was 13 ... N-R4 avoiding the main trouble from the continuation in the game.

14   N—N1!!

The manoeuvre R-B3 has been tried in a slightly different situation, but this is a quite unexpected idea in this kind of position. This paradoxical move, which seems to slow down proper development, is very strong and puts the black queen in danger again. Was it suggested by telephone from chess circles in Moscow, invented during the past day or two in Spassky's apartment at the 'Saga' hotel, or found over the board in those 30 minutes, as White himself claimed?

Whatever it was, it made an impression on an opponent who has never been in trouble with this line in his whole chess career. For almost the first time in the match, Fischer took more time on his clock than Spassky finding an answer.

14 ...   Q—N5

Not 14 ... Q-N7? 15 P-QR4! (15 P-QR3 R-B1! 16 N-B3 N-R4) and 16 N-R3! with the double threat N-B4 and KR-QN1. But 14 ... Q-R5 was an alternative; in case of 15 Q-K3 N-K2 Black can escape with the queen to QB3, but 15 P-B4 could build up new pressure in the centre.

15 Q—K3

Again cutting off avenues of escape from the black queen.

15 ...   P—Q4?

Black gives a pawn back in the hope of activating his pieces, but it is a wishful, positional solution, for White will obtain too much pressure in the centre. The alternative was 15 ... N-K2, to free the QB3 square for the queen's escape, but after 16 N(1)-Q2 (not 16 P-QR4 P-B4 17 N(1)-Q2 PxP 18 P-B3 because of ... N-Q4!) it is not clear that Black's position deserves much optimism! Is this, then, a refutation of the "poisoned pawn" line?

16 PxP   N—K2

17 P—B4!

Increasing the pressure in the centre. 17 PxP PxP would offer much more activity to Black's pieces.

17 ...   N—B4

The best, and almost the only good piece that Black has.

18 Q—Q3!

The most active square. The queen exercises pressure against the strong black knight: 18 ... PxP 19 PxP N-B4? 20 QxN BxB 21 N(1)-Q2 BxR 22 RxB would give White a strategic victory. The material is even and Black's only difficulties are having no safe place for the king, and the problem of how to complete his development satisfactorily. White has a clear plan of bringing fresh forces into the battlefield, and obviously stands much better!

18 ...   P—R5?

This speeds up the decision, but it is hard to blame Black for his lack of patience in a strategically lost position.

19 B—N4

Black was threatening 19 ... N-N6+ 20 PxN PxP+ 21 K-N1 B-B4+, but now there is an answer in 21 B-R3. At the same time, the black knight, his best piece, is under increased pressure.

19 ...   N—Q3

20 N(1)—Q2

20 PxP PxP 21 Q-N6+ K-K2! would not be effective. Black is helpless now against the growing pressure of White's pieces.

20 ...   P—B4?

It loses, but what else?

21 P—QR3!

The queen is in terrible trouble now.

21 ...   Q—N3

No other move: 21 ... Q-R5 22 N-B5.

22   P—B5!   Q—N4

Forced, again.

23   Q—QB3!

The threat 24 P-QR4 is deadly now.
black's queen has no good retreat, and his
KR is also attacked.

23   ...   PxB

23 ... R-KN1 24 P-R4 B-N2 25 N-Q4!
also wins easily.

24   P—QR4!   P—R6

The last desperate attempt. 24 ... Q-K7
25 QR-K1 wins the queen and keeps the
simultaneous attack on black's knight and
rook.

25	PxQ	PxP+
26	KxP	R—R6
27	Q—B6!	N—B4

27 ... B-K2 28 Q-N7 would be equally
hopeless.

28	P—B6!	B—B1
29	QPxP	BPxP
30	KR—K1	B—K2
31	RxKP	

Black resigns.

Fischer's lead was reduced to 6½:4½!

12

Bobby Fischer had settled down to play chess, and his complaints to the referee from time to time that 'there was a lot whispering in this room' were the sole remaining sign that he was not out of form. Lothar Schmid admitted once that there was always 'a grain of truth' in Fischer's demands, whatever 'torture' those could mean to other people. There was nothing wrong with Fischer asking for perfect conditions. So the German grandmaster did his best, pressing the button to light up the huge sign with the word 'Silence.' It could not stop one per cent. of the spectators whispering a little, but there was a small consolation for the challenger. In the passage behind the stage was a trolley, brought from Bobby's hotel, with three kinds of fish, meat, cheese and a selection of drinks. Spassky restricted his refreshment only to easily available fruit juices.

Bobby wanted to have a feast out of the twelfth game too, but Spassky did not wish to change his now honourable position in the match. The champion carefully chose an old line from the Twenties and Thirties, hoping that Fischer would not be well acquainted with its half forgotten secrets, and thus have an easy day before making a new attempt himself with the White pieces in the next game.

Fischer took more time than usual (he never plays the Queen's Gambit, it was said), but found the best moves. He obtained the advantage of the bishop pair, but the position was too simplified for him to be able to make much out of it. Spassky knew how to defend and was a confident man now.

Thus Spassky's idea was to disillusion Fischer's hope of a 'blitzkrieg' finish to the match, then the time would come to take the opportunities offered more abundantly by a disappointed opponent. Well planned or not, the atmosphere was different now and one sensed a long, exhausting fight for the title. This was short-lived.

White: Fischer
Black: Spassky
Queen's Gambit Declined, Orthodox Defence.
    1 P—QB4!
Alternating again! So, it was not just a psychological weapon for two games.
    1 ...   P—K3
Like Fischer, Spassky began to behave more casually. As usual Fischer was 7 minutes late, Spassky on time, but disappeared somewhere and returned to the stage with several minutes lost on his clock too. A new style in everything? Not quite. The move in the game indicates caution and patience.

2	**N—KB3**	**P—Q4**
3	**P—Q4**	**N—KB3**
4	**N—B3**	**B—K2**
5	**B—N5**	**P—KR3**
6	**B—R4**	**0—0**
7	**P—K3**	**QN—Q2!**

All this was played quickly by the opponents, but now Spassky did not want to repeat the Tartakower line which brought him defeat in the sixth game.

8	**R—B1**	**P—B3**
9	**B—Q3**	**PxP**
10	**BxP**	**P—QN4**

With the interpolated moves 5 ... P-KR3 and 6 B-R4 it was not a good moment for Capablanca's manoeuvre 10 ... N-Q4 anymore, because of 11 B-KN3! avoiding simplification.

11 B—Q3   P—R3

Preparing 12 ... P-B4, freeing Black's play. 12 ... P-N5? would waste a move and would permit 13 BxN! and 14 N-K4.

As far as one can recall, it is the first time that Spassky has used this variation of the Queen's Gambit, but this is also the first time Fischer has had to fight the wing development of black's QB. Spassky had the advantage of being able to choose the line in advance, and, by this juncture, Fischer had spent more time in deciding his plans.

12 P—QR4!

Although on little known ground, Fischer does not miss the best move. After 12 0-0 P-QB4 (not 12 ... B-N2? 13 BxN! NxB 14 N-K4) Black would equalize easily.

12 ...   PxP!

Also the best, obliging White to spend a move on recapturing the pawn, while after 12 ... P-N5? 13 BxN! and 14 N-K4 the QBP would be in trouble.

13 NxP   Q—R4+
14 N—Q2

Trying to maintain control of the important square QB5.

14 ...   B—N5

Preventing White from castling and threatening 15 ... BxN+. Weaker is 14 ... B-N2 15 0-0 QR-B1? 16 N-K4! and White won quickly in the game (which arose by a different order of moves) Taimanov-Jimenez, Palma de Mallorca 1970, which may be the only game with this same line in the last seven years!

15 N—B3

White was obliged to relax his pressure a bit on the crucial square QB5.

15 ...   P—B4

Without the text move Black could never get a reasonably good game. Theory considers all this to be the best play for both sides.

16 N—N3   Q—Q1

Defending the K-side again, but it is White who gains time now, for the black KB is misplaced. It was hard to find a good square for the black queen: 16 ... Q-R5!? 17 PxP NxP 18 NxN QxQ+ 19 KxQ! BxN 20 BxN PxB 21 N-Q5!, or 16 ... Q-R7 17 0-0 QxP 18 N-R4, or 16 ... Q-N3 17 PxP.

17 0—0   PxP
18 NxP   B—N2

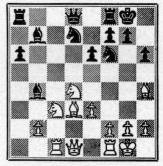

19 B—K4!

Fighting for the QB6 square for a white knight and threatening to weaken Black's K-side. Black is behind in development and faces difficulties.

19 ...   Q—N1!

Black had to do something to break the pin on the diagonal Q1-KR5 and to defend the bishop at the same time. After 19 ... Q-N3? 20 N-R4 Q-R2 21 R-B7 Black would be in danger of losing. The move in the game looks like the most reasonable choice.

20 B—N3

The alternative was 20 N-B6 BxN 21 BxB R-R2 22 B-N3.

20 ...   Q—R2

20 ... P-K4 would create weaknesses.

21 N—B6   B(N2)xN
22 BxB   QR—B1

White has the advantage of the bishop

pair, but it is not always decisive in a simple position.

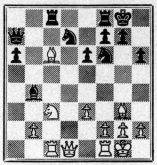

23 N—R4

Defending the stronghold on QB6 and thus maintaining some pressure along the open files. 23 Q-B3 was also playable.

23 ... KR—Q1

23 ... N-B4 24 NxN RxB? would not work well because of 25 N-K4! RxR 26 NxN+ seriously weakening Black's K-side.

24 B—B3

White wants to exchange one of the rooks and thus be able, more easily, to penetrate along one of the open files, but this manoeuvre is slow. 24 Q-B3 was a better alternative with the same purpose.

24 ... P—QR4!

Strengthening the position of the bishop and giving the queen more air. Not 24 ... N-K4? 25 BxN RxQ 26 RxR+ with a decisive material advantage.

25 R—B6

This is a logical consequence of the 24th move, but it is a vain hope to make Black more vulnerable along the QB-file after having forced the opponent to exchange a rook.

25 ... RxR
26 BxR R—QB1

This is a more sensitive file for Black, and it is sound defence to oppose on it. White's advantage is minimal.

27 B—B3 Q—R3!

Taking an important diagonal and activating the queen.

28 P—R3 Q—N4
29 B—K2 Q—B3
30 B—B3 Q—N4
31 P—N3!

Black's heavy pieces are more active and that makes chances even, but White is not satisfied with a draw by repetition of moves and so seeks to improve the position of his knight.

31 ... B—K2

Exercizing pressure on White's QN-pawn.

32 B—K2 Q—N5
33 B—R6 R—B3
34 B—Q3 N—B4!

This knight was passive too, and it is useful to get rid of the white knight which controls sensitive squares on the QB-file.

35 Q—B3!

The only way to worry his opponent.

35 ... R—B1

35 ... N(4)-K5 was playable.

36 NxN

Not 36 R-B1 Q-Q7! 37 RxN RxR 38 Q-R8+ B-B1 39 NxR Q-B8+ or 39 B-Q6 R-B8+ 40 K-R2 QxB.

36 ... BxN

Not 36 ... RxN? 37 Q-R8+ B-B1 38 B-Q6, and 36 ... QxN 37 Q-N7 would also be unpleasant.

37 R—B1 R—Q1

37 ... QxP? 38 RxB RxR 39 Q-R8+ was too obvious.

38 B—QB4

White had to defend the QNP this way: 38 Q-Q1 N-K5! Now Black must not play 38 ... P-R5? 39 PxP QxP 40 BxP.

38 ... Q—Q7
39 R—B1 B—N5
40 B—B7 R—Q2
41 Q—QB6

The sealed move.

41 ...   Q—B7

Black is in time to stop White's threat of P-K4-K5.

42   B—K5   R—Q7

An active defence. Black had to accept a slight weakening of his K-side.

43   Q—R8+   K—R2
44   BxN   PxB
45   Q—B3   P—B4
46   P—N4   Q—K5

Black had no time for 46 ... P-R5 47 PxBP RPxP 48 PxP QxB 49 QxP+ K-R1 50 R-R1 R-Q1 51 Q-B6+ and wins.

47   K—N2

There is not much for White in the endgame. But, as usual, the fight goes on.

47   ...   K—N3!

48   R—B1

Hoping for B-N5 and R-B7.

48   ...   B—R6

49   R—QR1

Not 49 R-B3? B-N7.

49   ...   B—N5
50   R—QB1   B—K2!

A little game of prestige: Black does not want a draw now. It is Black who is more active and the threat is 50 ... B-R5.

51   PxP+   PxP
52   R—K1

Ready to defend the second rank with 53 R-K2 and allowing the following small combination with a drawish endgame.

52   ...   RxP+
53   KxR   B—R5+
54   K—K2   QxQ+
55   KxQ   BxR
Draw agreed.

The score: 7:5 in favour of Fischer.

13

The novelty did not last long. Bobby badly wanted to be back where he was after the tenth game. He could not be shaken by anything. Hundreds of letters, which said that he was "a disgrace to the American people" or that he was "very handsome and elite" — did not touch him either. According to the magazine "Life", he said, blinking with an expression oddly like a baby owl's, "It's really surprising what people think about me." That was all.

Fischer wanted to be in shape, and he was. Having had three, then another two rows of front seats removed, he asked for another seven. But where, then, to put the spectators? He also asked that children with candy be forbidden to enter the hall because they made noise while unwrapping it. The referee Schmid felt slightly exhausted, mentioning to Fischer's representative, Fred Cramer, that the American side had by then submitted seven protests, while the Soviet side had made none. Cramer remained cool: "My job is to complain, not to approve." To an English newspaperman it looked like "the easiest job in the world."

Fischer was not shaken by the eleventh game. In the thirteenth one he simply switched to the Alekhine Defence. Strangely enough, once more Spassky was unprepared, although he should have known Fischer's game with the same line of two years before. Spassky was improvising at the board, and he did it badly. After only twelve moves, he was, as White, in a critical situation.

Fischer felt overconfident about his position. Although a pawn down, Spassky obtained strong pressure, but — while watching his clock — lacked resoluteness. The adjourned position looked hopeless. Yet, after twenty five minutes of reflection, he sealed the best move. Fischer did not like to see his opponent's salvation, and spent a sleepless night analysing the unexpectedly complicated position. According to Fischer's second, grandmaster Lombardy, "Fischer never before put so much energy into an endgame." Bobby was finally chased away to bed, by friends, at eight o'clock in the morning, and for the continuation in the early afternoon he was almost half an hour late.

The adjourned session was the most dramatic of the whole match. The home analysis went for some sixteen moves and Spassky came successfully out of his second period of time pressure. Instead of "an easy win" Fischer had to give up a piece for three pawns in order to keep uncertain winning chances. Spassky was nearing a drawish position when time pressure, coming for the third time in the game, took its toll. It was a terrible blow for the title-holder whose remaining hopes were vanishing.

White: Spassky
Black: Fischer
Alekhine Defence
1   P—K4!
Settling down to the new weapon from the eleventh game!
1   ...   N—KB3!
No Sicilian Defence this time! Well, Fischer has lately played the Alekhine Defence too, and Spassky, perhaps not!
2   P—K5   N—Q4
3   P—Q4   P—Q3
4   N—KB3
The sharpest line is 4 P—QB4 N—N3 5 P—B4.
4   ...   P—KN3
This has more edge to it than 4 ... B-N5. Larsen used to play 4 ... PxP!? 5 NxP P-KN3.
5   B—QB4
In the game Browne-Fischer, Rovinj/Zagreb 1970, 5 B-K2 B-N2 6 P-QB4 N-N3 7 PxP BPxP 8 N-B3 0-0 9 0-0 N-B3 10 B-K3 B-N5 11 P-QN3 P-Q4! was played.

5 N-N5 was fashionable for a while, but it might be premature because of 5 ... P-KB3! or 5 ... PxP 6 PxP B-N2 7 B-QB4 P-QB3, Vasyukov-Larsen, Moscow 1959.
5   ...   N—N3
In several tournament games 5 ... P-QB3 was played, but it is more passive and deprives Black of opportunities to strike back in the centre: 6 0-0 B-N2 7 PxP QxP 8 P-KR3 0-0, Kavalek-Kupka, Czechoslovakia 1968.
6   B—N3   B—N2

7   QN—Q2?!

After long reflection, Spassky finds something new, but it is not a happy solution, for there is a certain artificiality in the way in which White strengthens his outpost at K5. Keres used to play here 7 P-QR4 or 7 0-0 0-0 8 P-QR4 P-QR4 9 P-KR3 N-B3 10 Q-K2 P-Q4!? 11 N-B3 B-K3 12 B-KB4, Keres-Kupka, Kapfenberg 1970.

Interesting is 7 N-N5 and 8 P-KB4 securing better control of space.
7   ...   0—0
8   P-KR3?
Defending the KP even better, but before it was. attacked. It costs time, and one of the two moves, the 7th or the 8th, was superfluous.
8   ...   P—QR4!
By attacking the active, but exposed, bishop Black wants to provoke a weakening of White's Q-side, and thus obtain some additional squares for his minor pieces.
9   P—QR4?
White fights in the darkness and does not realize the danger he is in while meeting "energetically" the threat 9 ... P-R5. The move in the game, with the white knight on Q2, creates a serious weakness. White should have tried something more modest like 9 P-B3 B-B4 10 0-0 P-R5 11 B-B2 BxB 12 QxB N-B3 13 R-K1 PxP 14 NxP.
9   ...   PxP
10   PxP   N—R3!
Stressing the futility of White's strategy on the 7th move, when White defended before he was attacked. White's KB faces the unpleasant threat 11 ... N-B4 and white's QRP is even more in danger. Black has a big advantage, for White is also behind in development.
11   0—0
What else? 11 N-K4 QxQ+ 12 KxQ B-B4 13 N-N3 B-Q2 does not look promising.
11   ...   N—B4
12   Q—K2   Q—K1!
Aiming to win the pawn, at once!
13   N—K4   N(3)xP
14   BxN   NxB
15   R—K1
Typical of Spassky's reactions. White does not like the inferior game he would get if he tried to establish material equality by 15 Q-B4 B-Q2 16 QxQBP or 15 ... P-QN4

16 QxQBP B-B4, although it might have
been a better chance for a draw than
White's preferance for an attack, with
eventual counterchances for Black.

   15 ...   **N—N3**

Bringing the knight back to safety and
keeping his material advantage.

   16 B—Q2   **P—R5**
   17 B—N5

Trying his only chance to organize some
pressure, for 17 B-N4 N-Q4 was not good.

   17 ...   **P—R3**

Emphasizing what little power there was
in White's last move.

   18 B—R4

There is no other way to try to be active.

   18 ...   **B—B4!?**

Black misses the much better chance 18
... B-Q2! threatening 19 ... B-N4 and 20 ...
N-B5 and White would be in immediate
trouble. The threat from Black of ... P-KB4
would be very effective too.

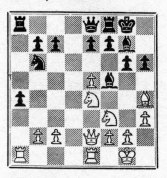

   19 P—KN4

White accepts the invitation to com-
mence an attack, for there is nothing better
that he can do.

   19 ...   **B—K3?**

Safer was 19 ... BxN 20 QxB P-QB3, and
again, better was 19 ... B-Q2 with the threat
20 ... P-KB4. Now, White gets a chance to
centralize a knight without having to pay
anything for it.

   20 N—Q4!   **B—B5**
   21 Q—Q2

It must have been disappointing for
Black, that White is not lost here. On the
contrary, he has counterplay, for 21 ... BxP
22 QxP B-N2 (otherwise 23 N-N5) 23 Q-K3

N-Q4 24 Q-Q2 would not be too pleasant
for Black.

   21 ...   **Q—Q2**
   22 QR—Q1

Black's careless play has given chances to
his opponent! The white KP is taboo and
exercises pressure against Black's K-side.

   22 ...   **KR—K1**
   23 P—B4!   **B—Q4**
   24 N—QB5   **Q—B1**
   25 Q—B3!?

25 P-K6! was strong and more dangerous. White probably did not like 25 ...
N-B5, but after 26 Q-B1 there would be
good counterplay ahead for him.

   25 ...   **P—K3!**

Stopping White's dangerous KP.

   26 K—R2

White is too slow. The approaching time
pressure makes its influence felt.

   26 ...   **N—Q2**

   27 N—Q3?

27 N-N5 was a better chance. Now,
Black is quick to obtain space for his
pieces.

   27 ...   **P—QB4!**
   28 N—N5   **Q—B3**
   29 N—Q6   **QxN**

29 ... KR-N1 30 Q-Q2 P-QN4 was
another possibility.

   30 PxQ   **BxQ**
   31 PxB   **P—B3**
   32 P—N5!

Doing his best in the struggle for black
squares.

   32 ...   **RPxP**
   33 PxP   **P—B4**
   34 B—N3   **K—B2**
   35 N—K5+   **NxN**

36   BxN

White's best chance is to play the inferior endgame with bishops of opposite colours.

36	...	**P—N4**
37	**R—KB1**	**R—R1!**

The threat R-B4-KR4 looks very unpleasant, and Black has to stop it.

38   B—B6!

The exchange is not worth taking. The bishop is a strong piece and may keep both black rooks busy.

38   ...   P—R6

Naturally, Black wants to keep the white rooks busy with his passed pawn.

39	**R—B4**	**P—R7**
40	**P—B4**	

Now was the first time that Spassky bent his head over the clock in order to check his flag. This important decision was made under extreme time pressure. 40 R-QR1 was the other choice to fight for a draw.

40	...	**BxP**
41	**P—Q7**	**B—Q4**
42	**K—N3!**	

The sealed move, and the best (as in the 7th game). White is threatening 43 R-KR4 RxR 44 KxR and then to capture the other black rook by promoting the QP.

42   ...   R—R6+

43   P—B3

Not 43 K-B2 R(6)xP! 44 P-Q8(Q) RxQ 45 BxR P-K4! winning the rook back.

43   ...   R(1)—R1!

The passive rook becomes an active piece.

44   R—KR4!   P—K4!

Getting air for the king and avoiding perpetual check.

45	**R—R7+**	**K—K3**
46	**R—K7+**	**K—Q3**
47	**RxP**	**RxP+**
48	**K—B2**	**R—B7+**
49	**K—K1**	

All forced and best play by both sides.

49	...	**KxP**
50	**R(5)xB+**	**K—B3**
51	**R—Q6+**	**K—N2**

51 ... K-B2 52 B-K5! would be dangerous. Black has begun a daring continuation, thanks to his excellent judgement that three pawns are still better than White's piece.

52   R—Q7+

52 R-K6 could be met by 52 ... R-QB1. Interesting was 52 R(6)-Q2 at once.

52   ...   K—R3

Not giving the opportunity for 53 B-Q8+.

53	**R(7)—Q2**	**RxR**
54	**KxR**	**P—N5**
55	**P—R4!**	

The only chance: 55 K-B2 K-N4 56 K-N2 P-QB5 57 K-R1 P-B6 would be hopeless.

55   ...   K—N4

56   P—R5   P—QB5!

Trying to gain a tempo in the race on opposite wings.

57   R—QR1

A must because of the threat 58 ... P-B6+ and P-R8(Q), for instance, 57 P-R6 P-B6+ 58 K-Q3 P-R8(Q) 59 RxQ RxR 60 P-R7 R-Q8+! 61 K-B2 R-KR8 62 P-R8(Q) RxQ 63 BxR K-B5 and Black wins with his three passed pawns on two sides.

57   ...   PxP

58   P—N6

This pawn wants to deprive black's rook of any activity.

58 ... P—R5

Black was thinking here of an interesting possibility to keep the rook active with 58 ... R-R6 59 P-N7 R-KN6 60 RxP P-B6+ 61 K-K2 P-N6 62 R-R8 but there is nothing clear for Black.

59 P—N7

59 BxP R-KN1 would favour Black.

59 ... P—R6
60 B—K7 R—KN1

Necessary to prevent the white pawn from queening.

61 B—B8

61 B-B6 was also playable: 61 ... P-R7 62 K-B2 K-B3 63 K-N2 K-Q3 64 R-R1! K-K3 65 B-Q4 K-Q4 66 B-B6 with a draw.

61 ... P—R7

If 61 ... P-B6+ 62 K-Q3!

62 K—B2 K—B3

The king must go to the other side or there is no chance to win.

63 R—Q1

Not allowing the king to cross the Q-file.

63 ... P—N6+
64 K—B3?

64 K-N2 was more precise: 64 ... P-B5 65 R-Q6+ K-B2 66 R-Q1! P-KB6 67 K-B3 P-B7 68 K-N2! with an easy draw, or 64 ... P-KR8(Q) 65 RxQ K-Q4 66 R-Q1+ K-K5 67 R-K1+! K-Q6 68 R-Q1+ K-K7 69 R-QB1 with a draw also.

64 ... P—KR8(Q)!

There lies Fischer's strength; Black made his move quickly having a clear vision that it was the only chance to fight for a win. After 64 ... P-B5 65 R-Q6+! K-B2 66 R-Q1!

Black's K-side pawns would be too far from the support of their king.

65 RxQ K—Q4
66 K—N2

White has to waste a move now because of his mistake on move 64.

66 ... P—B5
67 R—Q1+ K—K5
68 R—QB1 K—Q6

White was in time pressure now and had about four minutes left for four moves.

69 R—Q1+??

The last, and now decisive, mistake. After 69 R-B3+ K-Q5 70 R-B3 P-B6+ 71 K-R1 P-B7 72 RxBP+ K-B6 73 R-B3+ K-Q7 74 B-R3! White would easily salvage half a point.

69 ... K—K7!
70 R—QB1

White has lost two tempi now and cannot defend any more.

70 ... P—KB6
71 B—B5

A desperate try. Black's rook gets its freedom and that is decisive.

71 ... RxP
72 RxP R—Q2!

Again Black was quick in making this correct decision. Not 72 ... P-B7 73 BxP KxB 74 R-B4+! with chances for a draw. The threat ... R-Q8 (or ... R-Q7+ first) is deadly.

73 R—K4+ K—B8
74 B—Q4 P—B7

White resigns. There is a threat of 75 ... RxB, too.

The score: 8:5 for Fischer!

14

Fischer left the stage but Spassky, after having resigned the thirteenth game, remained seated. "It is very strange," he said (as though hypnotized) and tried to reconstruct the position of a few moves earlier. "How can one lose with the opponent's only rook locked in completely at KN1?

The shock was twofold: it gave Fischer what was perhaps a decisive advantage in points in the match. And on Sunday, August 13th, Spassky, according to the doctor's statement 'did not feel well', and the fourteenth game was postponed. There were rumours that Fischer was not happy about this and that he had even protested to FIDE in Amsterdam. True or not, it could not harm the champion's right to postpone three times during the match. If necessary, Spassky could postpone once more.

And so the match was not on for three days, and the chess show had to step in instead. Something was going on 'behind the scenes'. Apart from the episodic protest (not signed by Fischer) of Mr. Cramer to the president of FIDE in Amsterdam concerning the 'arrogance and incompetence' of the referee, Fischer's lawyer Paul Marshall asked that the loser's share of the prize fund (which was the minimum he could win) be deposited in advance at Kennedy Airport. When refused, Marshall compromised by suggesting the U.S. Embassy in Reykjavik as an alternative.

A spokesman of the Icelandic Chess Federation commented: 'We are willing to consider any reasonable demand, but we must know why they have asked this now — more than half way through the match!'

There could have been several 'becauses'. Barry Fredericks, who negotiated for exclusive movie rights for Chester Fox, flew to Iceland to discuss the deadlock. He was not granted a meeting with Fischer but discussed with an Icelandic attorney the possibilities of suing Fischer under Icelandic law. He said he might try to impound Fischer's share of the purse until some settlement was reached.

Paul Marshall, Fischer's lawyer, laughed this option off saying that Fredericks would have to 'use all his imagination on that one'. But he did not forget to add before his departure that Fischer still wanted the match filmed, but not by crews in the playing hall. Bobby wanted a number of television cameras installed in the hall under remote control from outside. "This is not a soccer match with people running back and forth. You do not need crews right in there," was Marshall's explanation.

To prove the seriousness of Fischer's intentions, he said that he had talked with Fischer until six o'clock in the morning, 'philosophizing about women and discussing financial offers. One major film company in California has offered Bobby a six-figure sum to advise on a spy-murder mystery based on chess'. Meanwhile, Chester Fox filmed a Yugoslav journalist who had a gift for mimicking Boris and Bobby at the chess table.

Instead of Sunday, the 13th, (an unlucky number for Spassky), the game was played on Tuesday, August 15th. In the meantime, Spassky's wife Larissa arrived from Moscow, and so did the wives of other members of Spassky's team, Geller, Krogius and Nei. The ladies stayed in the Soviet Embassy and did not intend to interfere with the match.

Boris opened modestly, waiting for Fischer to strike first. Bobby did, deviating from two previous games with the Queen's Gambit in spite of his successful play in those games. The position was to Spassky's liking and it was one of the rare occasions when he knew better than Bobby how to treat it. Realizing his sudden difficulties, Fischer hastened to play a simplifying continuation and blundered away a pawn. Spassky had even more reason to be tense inside and, like his rival, blundered a pawn back a few moves later. When Bobby instantly grabbed the black pawn Spassky turned in his swivel chair abruptly and, with his back to everyone, looked at the distant wall with a feeling of sheer disgust with himself. And so it was a draw, haughtily scorned by experts but liked by the spectators for its 'human touch'.

White: Fischer
Black: Spassky
Queen's Gambit Declined

1 P—QB4

The challenger has played this move in the match more frequently than his favourite 1 P-K4!

1	...	P—K3
2	N—KB3	P—Q4
3	P—Q4	N—KB3
4	N—B3	B—K2
5	B—B4!	

Deviating from the two previous games where White played 5 B-N5 entering lines of the Orthodox Defence. The move in this game has become fashionable in recent years.

5 ... 0—0

The alternative is 5 ... P-B4 6 QPxP N-R3 (or 6 ... Q-R4 7 N-Q2!) 7 B-Q6! (weaker could be 7 P-K3 NxP 8 PxP PxP 9 B-K2 0-0 10 0-0 B-K3 11 B-K5 R-B1 12 R-B1 P-QR3 P-QN4 14 B-Q3? P-Q5! winning the exchange, Petrosian-Spassky, 8th match game 1969) 7 ... NxP (or 7 ... PxP 8 Q-Q4! 0-0 9 P-K4 N-Q2 10 BxP N(3)xP 11 R-Q1 BxB 12 QxB with the better game, Portisch-Ivkov, Prague 1970) 8 BxB QxB 9 PxP PxP 10 P-K3 0-0 11 B-K2 N(4)-K5 12 Q-Q4 with some advantage, Portisch-Bobotzov, Amsterdam 1971.

6 P—K3 P—B4

The logical counter in the centre, since White has less pressure there with his QB not on KN5.

Interesting is 6 ... P-QN3, or 6 ... QN-Q2 7 P-QR3 P-B3 8 P-R3 P-QR3 9 P-B5 P-QN3! 10 P-QN4 P-QR4 11 B-Q3 B-R3 with an even game. Larsen-Spassky, Palma de Mallorca 1968.

7 QPxP N—B3

More flexible than 7 ... BxP 8 Q-B2 N-B3 9 P-QR3 Q-R4 10 R-Q1 B-K2 11 N-Q2 P-K4 12 B-N5 P-Q5 13 N-N3 and Black had to gamble by offering pawns. Portisch-Spassky, Havana 1966; or 7 ... Q-R4 8 R-B1 BxP 9 N-Q2 B-K2 10 B-K2 N-B3 11 0-0 Q-Q1 12 PxP NxP 13 NxN PxN 14 N-N3 with better chances for White. Larsen-Lombardy, Monte Carlo 1967.

8 PxP PxP

9	B—K2	BxP
10	0—0	B—K3

10 ... P-Q5 would be met by 11 N-QR4.

11 R—B1

Trying to make the black KB feel uncomfortable on its active square.

11	...	R—B1
12	P—QR3	P—KR3
13	B—N3	

Not yet 13 NxP QxN 14 QxQ NxQ 15 RxB NxB 16 PxN because of 16 ... N-Q5! 17 R-K5 NxB+ 18 RxN B-B5 winning the exchange. The move in the game also introduces the possibility of pinning with B-R4.

13 ...   B—N3!

Removing the bishop from the exposed square. Now the threat is 13 ... P-Q5. In case of 14 N-QR4 Black might reply in the centre with 14 ... N-K5.

14 N—K5

Hoping to diminish the effect of the possible break ... P-Q5, by reducing the number of pieces on the board. The isolated pawn gives free play to Black's pieces, but with the lesser number of pieces its weakness would become more apparent. Therefore, Black avoids the exchange of knights with his next move.

14 ...   N—K2!

In case of 14 ... P-Q5 15 NxN RxN 16 PxP BxP, 17 N-B3 could be unpleasant. Now the idea is an eventual ... N-B4.

15 N—R4

Not leaving Black's bishop in peace on its strong diagonal.

15 ...   N—K5

The natural reaction in the centre to White's wing manoeuvre.

16	RxR	BxR
17	N—KB3	

17 B-R4 B-B2 18 N-KB3 B-Q2 would be quite playable for Black. With the move in the game White increases his control of the blockading square Q4, and removes the knight from an exposed, inefficient post.

17 ...   B—Q2

In case of 17 ... B-B2 18 BxB QxB, Black would not be able to make use of the position of White's knight on the wing because of 19 Q-B1! With the move in the game Black aims to be the first to arrive on the QB-file.

18 B—K5?

18 NxB QxN 19 B-K5 was a good solution, keeping some advantage.

18 ...   BxN!

19 QxB   N—QB3

Black is now comfortable and more active. White has played around with his pieces, misjudging the result of the time-consuming manoeuvre that was his 18th move.

20 B—KB4

20 B-Q4 NxB 21 NxN Q-B3 would give Black an easy game.

20 ...   Q—B3

This natural move increases the pressure along two intersecting dark diagonals. Black now has the initiative!

21 B—QN5?

White, with his quick perception, has realized the dangers. But here he makes an oversight in his wish to simplify in an unnecessary rush. Yet, in a way, Fischer's instinct was tremendous. After the normal 21 Q-B2, 21 ... P-N4 22 B-N3 P-KR4 could be very unpleasant.

21	...	QxP
22	BxN	N—B6!

The flaw in White's rapid calculation.

23 Q—N4

Not 23 B-K5 NxQ 24 BxQ PxB! and Black would have a more mobile pawn majority than in the game.

23	...	QxQ
24	PxQ	PxB

24 ... N-K7+ 25 K-R1 NxB 26 BxNP would offer nothing. White's best hope, a pawn down, is to control the mobility of Black's pawns.

25	B—K5	N—N4
26	R—B1	R—B1?!

Less precise than 26 ... P-B3 gaining a tempo.

27 N—Q4

White is dreaming of entering a rook endgame with excellent drawing chances.

27 ... P—B3??

A terrible blunder in return and the position is now a draw. After 27 ... NxN (or BxN) 28 BxN (or respectively BxB) 28 ... P-B3 (Black would also have to keep a minor piece on the board, for after 28 ... BxB 29 PxB R-N1 30 K-B1 RxP 31 RxP RxP 32 R-R6 White could salvage a draw in the rook endgame, being only a pawn down) and 29 ... K-B2, Black would have a long but perhaps successful fight for a win.

28 BxP BxN

28 ... PxB 29 NxN offers Black nothing.

29	BxB	NxB
30	PxN	R—N1
31	K—B1	

This is the right order of moves: 31 RxP would be a little dangerous because of 31 ... P-QR4!

31	...	RxP
32	RxP	RxP
33	R—R6	K—B2
34	RxP+	K—B3
35	R—Q7	P—R4
36	K—K2	P—N4
37	K—K3	R—K5+
38	K—Q3	K—K3
39	R—KN7	K—B3
40	R—Q7	K—K3

Draw agreed.

The score remained intact: 8½:5½ in favour of Fischer.

15

At last Chester Fox announced the amount of money which he, because of Fischer's anti-filming attitude, was not going to earn: one million, two hundred and fifty thousand dollars! So what? Even if Fischer was sued, how could he afford to pay it?

Well, another cosmic age has dawned for chess grandmasters. Fischer's lawyer brought better news from the United States: with a few signatures, Bobby could make one million two hundred thousand in only three weeks after the match. But will he ever sign? One recalls a private episode after Fischer's match with Petrosian. Robert James Fischer was tempted with a six-figure sum to advertise a hair lotion. After a little hesitation, he rejected the offer with an argument of annihilating effect: 'I cannot do it. After all, I never use it!'

A reader of 'Time' magazine wrote to the Editor: 'To some people Bobby Fischer is impudent, arrogant, self-serving and somewhat childish. They are probably right, but do they know that he has to be rated one of the most brilliant chess masters of all time? Do they know that he alone has probably brought more prize money and better playing condiitions to tournament chess than all the greats combined?'

Fischer remained undisturbed by everything and went his own way. Now, he began complaining about the air-conditioning, the autograph hounds, the 'excessive spectator noise', and asked for the fifteenth game to be played in the back-stage room. Not again!

Horrifying memories of the forgotten past and the third game of the match came back. Knowing the rules and what Spassky's reaction would now be, Lothar Schmid made a nice little speech to the public before starting the chess clock on the stage, praying within himself for the best reaction from Bobby. That evening, referee Schmid, while sitting quietly at the dinner table, produced his normal statement in his usual tired voice:'I cannot move. I feel finished.'

It had been like that for two months, but everyone had survived, including the players, going through the hell of the fifteenth game. Boris, rumoured before to be suffering from defeatism, professed a new found determination: 'The first half of this match was not very interesting for me. The second half will be.' Indeed, he was a tougher opponent in the opening, too, and it was Fischer who spent more time in the beginning of the game.

When Fischer, with some delay, accepted the challenge of playing another Sicilian defence, Spassky applied the most up-to-date method of quick development against Fischer's favourite set-up in the Najdorf variation. Something took Fischer by surprise and he had to give up a pawn. But he succeeded in placing his minor pieces on their ideal squares. Thinking that being a pawn up was worth more than this achievement of Black's, Spassky avoided a draw by repetition of moves and then was almost on the brink of disaster.

Fischer played fast. No one knew whether it was the inspiration of genius or the impatience of being so close to his life's goal. Spassky found miraculous replies while in time pressure and on the next day Fischer did not find anything better than repeating moves. One could have predicted this outcome on the evening after the first session, when Fischer's second Lombardy was seen in his hotel unexpectedly looking for a table-tennis partner.

White: Spassky
Black: Fischer
Sicilian Defence
   1 P—K4
Being three points behind, the title holder now had no better weapon than king's pawn, in order to put to a severe test Fischer's double-edged lines.
   1 ...   P—QB4!
In the thirteenth game, Black had not tried his favourite defence.
   2 N—KB3   P—Q3
   3 P—Q4   PxP
   4 NxP   N—KB3
   5 N—QB3   P—QR3!
Fortune favours the bold.
   6 B—KN5!
Spassky's challenge is now complete.
   6 ...   P—K3
   7 P—B4   B—K2!
Black is first to deviate from the eleventh game, expressing no wish for the risky "poisoned pawn" line (7 ... Q-N3).
   8 Q—B3   Q—B2
   9 0—0—0   QN—Q2
Giving additional support to Black's KN: 9 ... P-N4? would be premature because of 10 BxN BxB 11 BxP+! PxB 12 N(4)xNP with a devastating attack.
   10 B—Q3!
The most recently discovered method for White who is going straight for the attack along the central files. Unclear is 10 B-K2 P-N4 11 BxN NxB 12 P-K5 B-N2 13 Q-N3 (13 PxN BxQ 14 BxB BxP 15 BxR BxN 16 RxB P-Q4 17 BxP PxB 18 R-K1+ K-B1 holds for Black) PxP 14 PxP (Velimirovic-Bronstein, Vinkovci 1970), when with 14 ... N-Q2 Black could have kept the chances even. Frequently played and very much explored is 10 P-KN4, but Fischer has met that move several times in his tournament praxis and he could not be surprised by anything in that line.
   10 ...   P—N4
   11 KR—K1

This is the idea, to bring all his forces into play as quickly as possible and eventually to open the K-file.
   11 ...   B—N2
11 ... P-N5 has also been played and may be stronger e.g. 12 N(B3)-K2 N-B4 with an equal game, Mikenas-Aronin, 24th USSR Championship, or 12 N-Q5 PxN 13 PxP which is unclear according to Pachman but probably unsound in view of the Velimirovic-Ljubojevic game mentioned below.

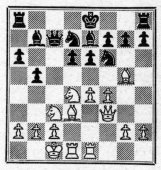

   12 Q—N3!
Not quite unknown, but still a new idea. In this position the sacrifice 12 N-Q5!? has attracted the attention of aggressive tournament competitors. In the game Jimenez-Mecking, Palma Interzonal 1970, after 12 N-Q5 PxN 13 N-B5 B-B1 (much more interesting is 13 ... K-B1) White missed a chance to destroy his opponent with 14 P-K5! PxP 15 PxP NxP 16 NxP+! BxN 17 BxN.

In the Velimirovic-Ljubojevic game mentioned above play continued: 12 N-Q5? NxN 13 PxN BxB 14 RxP+ PxR 15 NxKP and now, with 15 ... Q-N3! Black could have left his opponent with insufficient compensation for the material sacrificed and consolidated his position within a few moves.

With the move in the game White does
not commit himself to material sacrifices,
but improves the position of his queen
which now exercises pressure along the
KN-file. White played all his moves quickly
and was obviously ready for this line. In
contrast, Fischer had to spend more time
on his replies.

12 ...   0—0—0

Removing his king into safety. After 12
... P-N5, 13 N-Q5! could be played with
even more effect because of the improved
position of White's queen and its pressure
along the KN-file. The idea of the knight
sacrifice is to open the K-file and attack
straight away, but now the black king has
escaped.

13 BxN

The logical consequence of White's 12th
move, played in order to exploit the pressure along the KN-file. White took a long
time over his 13th move, perhaps surprised that Black could castle long.

13 ...   NxB

Black had no better reply. On 13 ... BxB
14 BxP! PxB (14 ... BxN 15 BxN+) 15
N(4)xNP and 16 NxP+ would follow with a
winning game; and after 13 ... PxB 14 Q-N7
(14 P-B5 is also playable) QR-B1 15
NxKP! White would again win material.

With the move in the game, Black may
hope for some counterplay as compensation for the lost pawn.

14 QxP   QR—B1

Not 14 ... KR-N1 15 QxBP QR-B1 16
QxP+.

15 Q—N3

The queen had to be brought back to
safety.

15 ...   P—N5

Using his chance for an attempt to
disrupt the collaboration of White's pieces.

16 N—R4

The only active reply. Black has still to
prove whether he has sufficient compensation for his material disadvantage.

16 ...   KR—N1

17 Q—B2

After 17 Q-B3 P-Q4 18 P-K5 N-K5 19
BxN PxB Black would win a tempo.

17 ...   N—Q2!

Fischer knows many positions, but this
one especially well. Black protects the

squares on the queen side and threatens 18
... N-B4. Black is trying to make use of the
wing position of White's QN, and that is his
best chance.

18 K—N1!

Meeting the threat of 18 ... Q-R4 19 P-
QN3 N-B4.

18 ...   K—N1!

Both players are far sighted. If 18 ... N-
B4 19 NxN PxN (19 ... QxN is playable but
it would not offer anything substantial) 20
N-B3 QxP (if 20 ... P-B5 21 B-B1 QxP 22
BxP; or 21 ... P-B6 22 Q-R7!) 21 Q-K2!
Black would regain material equality, but
with a bad position because of his light
square weaknesses.

19 P—B3!

Wishing to open the QB-file and leaving
the square QB2 free for his bishop.

19 ...   N—B4

19 ... PxP 20 R-QB1 would not be attractive for Black.

20 B—B2   PxP

Not 20 ... NxN 21 BxN PxP 22 R-QB1
Q-R4 23 B-B6! PxP 24 QxP!

21 NxBP   B—KB3

A strange position has arisen. Black has
placed his minor pieces on the ideal squares
for the Najdorf variation, but, at the same
time, he is a pawn down. Is he lost or has he
even chances? It is hard to guess, even for
an expert.

22 P—KN3   P—KR4

Insisting on making Black's KR an
active piece. White now decides to break,
having no other possibility for developing
immediate activity.

23 P—K5!?

It looks attractive, but is actually

double-edged. What else could White do to prove his superiority? Perhaps 23 R-QB1.

23 ...   PxP
24 PxP   B—KR1!

An original solution, keeping the pressure on White's weak K-pawn which could not be captured at once by 24 ... BxP because of 25 N(4)-N5! PxN 26 NxP Q-N3 (not 26 ... BxKNP 27 PxB Q-N3 28 Q-B4+ K-R1 29 N-B7+ K-R2 30 R-K3) 27 RxB with a big advantage.

25 N—B3   R—Q1

25 ... BxN 26 QxB BxP 27 N-R4 would leave Black's king more open. White was threatening 26 N-K4 with a positionally won game, so with his last move Black had to fight for the central file.

26 RxR+   RxR
27 N—KN5

This does not bring much, but there is nothing else to do: 27 Q-K2 BxN 28 QxB BxP would be slow now, for Black has the Q-file.

27 ...   BxP
28 QxP

Not 28 NxBP R-KB1.

28 ...

The best that White can do now is to repeat moves with 29 Q-K8+ R-Q1 (otherwise 30 NxP) 30 Q-B7, but he is not satisfied with such an outcome and takes a terrible risk. 28 ... BxP 29 PxB QxP also worked, 30 R-Q1 QxN with an even game.

29 QxRP?!   BxN

Using his chance to weaken the position of White's king, while the other white pieces are far away.

30 PxB   Q—N3+

31 K—B1

31 K-R1 would be safer if it were possible, but then 31 ... R-Q7 would follow with very unpleasant threats.

31 ...   Q—R4
32 Q—R8+

Not 32 NxP?? N-Q6+ (or N-N6+) winning the queen.

32 ...   K—R2

Black has a very strong attack and the two pawns down do not count.

33 P—QR4

Now it was White who was in worse time pressure. 33 K-N2 R-Q7 would be very unpleasant, and 33 Q-K5 R-Q4 did not work either. Black's attack is extremely dangerous.

33 ...   N—Q6+

Going for the simplest solution, clearing away a piece which defends White's king. Unclear would be 33 ... NxP 34 BxN QxB 35 Q-K5 and there is no mating net, for Black needs a move or two to prepare it, and his own king might be irreparably exposed to checks in the meantime.

34 BxN   RxB

Everything in White's position is now hanging, two pawns around the king and the knight on KN5. White makes the only move which defends part of his set up.

35 K—B2   R—Q4

After 35 ... R-Q1 36 Q-K5 QxP+ 37 K-B1 the identical position would be reached as if Black had played 33 ... NxP 34 BxN QxB 35 Q-K5. Perhaps this was still the best chance to win after 37 ... Q-R8+ 38 K-B2 Q-R7+ (38 ... B-K5+ does not bring a definite result) 39 K-B1 Q-Q7+ 40 K-N1 R-Q4 41 Q-K3+ QxQ 42 RxQ RxN 43 RxP R-KB4, and the presence of rooks on the board could eventually make the outcome of the game different from the otherwise drawish endgame (bishop of the wrong colour for the black rook pawn).

36 R—K4!

As in several previous difficult situations, Spassky finds a marvellous resource. This move is the only one left to keep any chances of salvaging half a point.

36 ...   R—Q1

On 36 ... RxN, 37 Q-Q4+ would follow, and after the exchange of queens White would also have a QR-pawn and a more active king than in the position which could have arisen on moves 33 and 35.

37 Q—N7

This is the best position that White could reach.

37 ...   Q—KB4

This pin looks more unpleasant than White's. 37 ... Q-Q4 would not win because of 38 R-Q4.

38 K—N3

Trying another resource.

38 ...   Q—Q4+

Trying to bring his pieces closer to Spassky's king, but it does not bring anything decisive. An unclear chance was 38 ... K-R1 39 Q-K5 BxR 40 QxB+ Q-Q4+! 41 QxQ+ PxQ or 41 P-B4 QxQ 42 NxQ P-K4!, but the real continuation should have been 38 ... R-Q8! 39 P-KR4 Q-B7! bringing the heavy pieces behind the White king.

39 K—R3   Q—Q7

With the idea of 40 ... R-Q2 and 41 ... Q-B8+, but it also turns out not to be effective.

40 R—QN4   Q—B8+

The game was adjourned here and White sealed the obvious move.

41 R—N2   Q—R8+
42 R—R2   Q—B8+

In case of 42 ... Q-Q8 43 R-QN2 R-Q2 44 Q-K5! Black cannot do much, for his bishop is tied down by White's mating threat on QN8.

43 R—N2   Q—R8+

Draw! The resumption of the game did not take more than 2 minutes, but the spectators were grateful even for that much and applauded loudly. Of course, the players could have agreed on a draw by telephone, but Fischer probably had his own reasons for not doing so.

The lead was still intact: 9:6 in favour of Fischer! How much closer to the title is he?

16

At last the reporters were happy. They heard that Fischer had a date with a lady. But that was a bad joke as the lady was a judge from New York High Court, who wanted to freeze Fischer's royalties until his case with Chester Fox was legally solved. Kindly, smiling Mr. Fox, while moving around in the tournament hall, was dead serious. Thanks to Bobby, he had plenty of free time and therefore, even examined the possibility of suing Fischer not only in New York, but in Reykjavik, as well.

When 'seeds of suspicion' were thrown, making the Icelandic Chess Federation appear to be involved in the case too, the hosts produced their statement. Their indignation was as deep as the list of signatures on the declaration that 'it is not and has at no moment been the slightest intention of the Icelandic Chess Federation to sue Mr. Robert Fischer.' Not only the president, but the vice-president, the secretary, the treasurer and another member of the Federation made a joint testimony on the subject.

So, it was only Chester Fox who was suing the challenger 'for huge amounts'. Was it the publicity that pleased the film director? For, he looked too happy for a man who was losing so much money. Was Fischer concerned now for the income in the United States from his two books? But, he never signs anything! Life is not chess, and Bobby needed plenty of time to think things over. If he ever could. Other people were quick to sign for him contracts of whose contents he was never quite certain. So, how could he accept them? And, they used to betray him, like those promises of 'technological progress' and of invisible cameras, and, then, what did he see? There were two huge towers with 'hidden' cameras on the stage by the very beginning of the match!

Chester Fox, himself, former prize-winner for a documentary film, recorded on a celluloid tape for posterity Fischer's astonishment on seeing strange wooden constructions on either side of the chess table. The Greek horse in Troy certainly looked much better! If Fox had no true reason to be cross with Fischer, Spassky did have.

This was disclosed by the ending of this game when Boris was a pawn up and dragged on a hopelessly drawish position for another hour or two and another 25 moves, so that Bobby, after having signed the inevitable result on a score sheet, left the stage like the wind. Was it retaliation for the previous day when Bobby made Spassky come to the hall in order to sit there for only two minutes and agree on an obvious draw in the adjourned position? Or, was it something else, that had occurred in abundance during the match and had accumulated to the point where Spassky decided to give a lesson on basic chess endings to the several thousand attentive onlookers?

Whatever it was, it looked as if 'Spassky was rude to Fischer' — the feeling expressed by the surprised Fischer's second, grandmaster Lombardy. Fischer, by now, could have been annoyed even by Spassky's constantly 'too quiet attitude'

(!), while Bobby was 'left to fight alone for better playing conditions'. That coughing, for instance! Fischer protested twice during the game and asked that the players be moved to the back-stage room, but in vain. The challenger even pointed at a written protest in his pocket, but refrained from showing it to the referee, waiting for a better opportunity on some other day. His only bitter remark about the coughing was: 'They should go to the hospital, not to the world championship match!'

The sixteenth game illustrated Spassky's newly found ability to keep Fischer at a distance. Perhaps, White even overlooked the temporary sacrifice of the rook and therefore wanted to reduce the game to a draw as soon as possible. But Spassky failed to stretch his hand for an armistice at the proper moment, and used his symbolic material advantage for a little psychological torture.

White: Fischer
Black: Spassky
Ruy Lopez
   1   P—K4

Since the tenth game, Fischer had not opened with his favourite KP.
   1 ...   P—K4

Although it is a different opening, it is the same cautious approach by Black as in the 14th game.
   2   N—KB3   N—QB3
   3   B—N5   P—QR3
   4   BxN

Faithful to his tactics not to repeat the same line twice. This differs from the tenth game where 4 B-R4 was played. Fischer surprised the world with the Exchange Variation in the Olympiad at Havana 1966 and had excellent results with it there. But, it could not be a surprise to Spassky now.
   4 ...   QPxB
   5   0—0

This move poses more problems for Black than does an immediate 5 P-Q4, and Nimzovich is once more proved right in his pronouncement that the threat is stronger than its execution. Though White has sold his strong bishop for a knight, a bishop which is usually Black's main strategical problem in many variations of the Lopez, there is no basic flaw in White's tactics. He has gained a tempo for development, somewhat spoiled Black's pawn structure and revived the threat to Black's KP.
   5 ...   P—B3

In the game Andersson-Portisch, Las Palmas 1972, Black tried the less usual 5 ... Q-Q3 and after 6 P-Q4 (playable is 6 P-Q3

or 6 P-QN3) PxP 7 NxP B-Q2 8 N-QB3 0-0-0 9 B-K3 N-R3 10 P-KR3 P-KN4 11 Q-R5 P-N5 12 N-B5 NxN 13 PxN PxP 14 QR-Q1 Q-N5 15 B-N5 B-K2 16 P-QR3 Q-B4 17 BxB QxB 18 KR-K1 P-R7+ 29 KxP Q-B4 20 QxBP QxP(B7) had strong counterplay.
   6   P—Q4

White traded the bishop pair hoping to have a more effective pawn majority on the K-side in the endgame.
   6 ...   B—KN5

An active reply. The alternative is 6 ... PxP 7 NxP! (7 QxP QxQ 8 NxQ P-QB4 would deprive White of a gain of tempo with the rook on Q1, as in the game Fischer-Portisch quoted below) with some advantage for White:

1) 7 ... P-QB4 8 N-N3 QxQ 9 RxQ B-Q3 10 N-R5! P-QN4 11 P-QB4 (weaker is 11 P-QR4 N-K2 12 N-B3 R-QN1, Perez-Spassky, Havana 1962) N-K2 12 B-K3 P-B4 13 N-B3 P-B5 14 P-K5! BxP 15 BxQBP BxN 16 PxB N-N3 17 N-B6 with a better endgame. Fischer-Portisch, Havana 1966;

2) 7 ... B-Q3 8 Q-R5+ P-KN3 9 Q-B3 BxP+ 10 KxB QxN 11 R-Q1 Q-R5 12 B-B4 Q-B2 13 Q-QN3! QxQ 14 RPxQ B-K3 15 BxP with a superior endgame. Hecht-Gligoric, Teesside 1972;

3) 7 ... N-K2 8 B-K3 N-N3 9 N-Q2! B-Q3 10 N-B4 0-0 11 Q-Q3 N-K4 12 NxN BxN 13 P-KB4 B-Q3 14 P-B5! Q-K2 15 B-B4 BxB 16 RxB B-Q2 17 R-K1 Q-B4 18 P-B3 QR-K1 19 P-KN4 Q-Q3 20 Q-N3 R-K2 21 N-B3 with a big positional advantage because of the threat P-K5. Fischer-Unzicker, Siegen 1970.

7 PxP

This can lead to a sharp endgame. Playable is 7 P-B3 B-Q3 (weaker is 7 ... PxP 8 PxP Q-Q2 9 P-KR3 B-K3 — or 9 ... B-R4 10 N-K5 BxQ 11 NxQ KxN 12 RxB R-K1 13 P-B3 N-K2 14 N-B3 K-B1 15 B-K3 P-KB4 16 QR-B1 PxP 17 PxP Fischer-Jimenez, Havana 1966 — 10 N-B3 0-0-0 11 B-B4! N-K2 12 R-B1 N-N3 13 B-N3 B-Q3 14 N-QR4! BxB? 15 PxB K-N1 16 N-B5 Q-Q3 17 Q-R4 K-R2? 18 NxRP! and White won, Fischer-Gligoric, Havana 1966) 8 B-K3 N-R3! intending 9 ... N-B2 as in the game Hort-Gligoric, Sousse 1967.

7 ...   QxQ
8 RxQ   PxP

Playable is 8 ... BxN (in order to spoil White's pawn mass, too) 9 PxB PxP:

1) 10 P-KB4 N-B3! 11 PxP NxP 12 B-K3 B-B4 13 N-Q2 NxN 14 BxB 0-0-0 and Black won the ending, having pressure on the central files and the possibility of blocking White's central pawns. Lee-Gligoric, Hastings 1965/66;

2) 10 B-K3 B-Q3 11 N-Q2 N-K2 12 N-B4 0-0-0 13 R-Q3 P-QN4 14 N-R5 B-N5 15 N-N3 RxR 16 PxR N-N3 17 K-B1 R-B1 18 K-K2 N-B5+ 19 BxN RxB 20 R-KN1 R-R5 21 RxP RxP 22 P-R3 B-Q3 23 P-B4! PxP 24 P-Q4 K-Q1 25 N-R5 P-B4 26 P-K5 B-B1 27 N-B6+ K-K1 28 RxBP and Black resigned. Fischer-Rubinetti, Buenos Aires 1970.

9 R—Q3

Avoiding the weakening of the pawn structure now. This was also played in the game Fischer-Smyslov, Monte Carlo 1967.

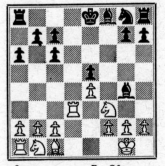

9 ...   B—Q3!
This is a known improvement. After 9 ... BxN 10 RxB N-B3 11 N-B3 B-N5 12 B-N5

BxN 13 PxB! (Fischer's idea!) R-KB1 (13 ... NxP 14 R-K1 with a superior endgame) 14 BxN RxR 15 RxR PxR 16 R-Q1 K-K2 17 R-Q3 and Black had difficulties in the endgame, because White's pawn majority on the K-side was more dangerous than Black's on the opposite wing. Fischer-Smyslov, Monte Carlo 1967.

10 QN—Q2   N—B3
11 N—B4   NxP
12 N(4)xP

This is better than 12 N(3)xP B-K3 with a satisfactory game. Hecht-Matanovic, Berlin 1971.

12 ...   BxN(B3)

Wasting no time on trying to preserve the bishop pair. 12 ... B-KB4 13 P-KN4 would not work well, anyhow, because of White's threat of R-K3.

13 NxB   0—0

Black has a comfortable development, and White's only advantage lies in the possibility of activating his pawn majority in the K-side. For the moment, this goal is still far away.

14 B—K3   P—QN4!

Using the black pawns to obtain — if nothing else — more space on the Q-side, and then eventually to threaten the retarded white pawns there.

15 P—B4!?
Meeting the action of Black and wanting to block the black pawns. The strategic idea is the right one, but its execution is slightly premature. 15 R-QB1 was playable.

15 ...   QR—N1
Increasing the strength of the QN-pawn outpost.

16   R—QB1   PxP

There is no hope of doing anything with the doubled QB-pawns, and rather than wait till the position becomes frozen on the Q-side, Black opens the file there. White wished for the opposite, a blocked situation on the Q-side, and then to turn his attention to the king's wing where he feels stronger.

17   R—Q4

Necessary. Of course not 17 RxP? RxP 18 RxN?? R-N8+.

17   ...   KR—K1

Maintaining the knight in its strong position in the centre. White therefore forces the exchange of a piece with his next move.

18   N—Q2   NxN

19   RxN

Now, the White rooks can move better and try to protect the pawns on the Q-side. The crucial problem is whether Black — with his temporary initiative — can prevent White from consolidating his Q-side. Otherwise, Black's pawn weaknesses would be a dangerous disadvantage.

19   ...   R—K5!

The consequent continuation after the exchange of knights. The rook occupies the same square. 19 ... B-K4 20 RxP RxP (or BxP) 21 RxR BxR 22 RxP would be pleasant for White. Black has to sell his QB5-pawn at a dearer price.

20   P—KN3

20 K-B1 was not possible because of 20 ... BxP! (it would be a capture of a different kind to the one we saw in the first game of the match for if 21 P-KN3 then 21 ... BxP). The move in the game also takes the square KB5 from the black bishop, and kills the mating threats on White's back rank.

20   ...   B—K4

If White's king approaches the centre, this move would not be possible later.

21   R(1)—B2

Stubbornly defending pawns on the Q-side.

21   ...   K—B2

Activating the king, and preparing a small combination. White does the same with his king, relying on the unpleasant threat 23 K-B3.

22   K—N2   RxP!

A sudden tactical thrust. The point is that if 23 R-Q7+ Black has an answer in K-K3, now attacking the rook and keeping the material balance. The good side of Black's move is also that it diminishes the number of White pawns without having to play 22 ... P-B6 23 PxP and thus allow White the more favourable pawn formation.

23   K—B3

The best solution. After 23 RxR P-B6 24 R-Q7+ K-K3 White would be in danger of losing.

23   ...   P—B6

Freeing the fifth rank for the rook. The simplifications are inevitable now.

24   KxR   PxR

25   RxQP

All forced.

25   ...   R—N4

Without rooks, White would feel easier with his good control of white squares. White recaptures the pawn with his next move.

26   R—B2   B—Q3

27   RxP   R—QR4

Keeping the rook more active. Therefore, White decides to enter a drawish endgame with his next offer of exchanging bishops.

28   B—B4   R—R5+

29   K—B3   R—R6+

29 ... BxB 30 PxB would not change matters at all.

30   K—K4   RxRP

31   BxB   PxB

32   RxQP   RxP

33   RxP   RxP

Black is a pawn up, but it is a theoretical draw, known from tuition books. Two pawns against one on the same side cannot win in the rook endgame with correct play.

34 K—B3

Avoiding the danger of the White king being cut from the pawns. The rest of the game is unnecessary and the only interest is its unusual length.

34	...	R—Q7
35	R—R7+	K—B3
36	R—R6+	K—K2
37	R—R7+	R—Q2
38	R—R2	K—K3
39	K—N2	R—K2
40	K—R3	K—B3
41	R—R6+	R—K3
42	R—R5	P—R3
43	R—R2	K—B4
44	R—B2+	K—N4
45	R—B7	P—N3

46	R—B4	P—R4
47	R—B3	R—KB3
48	R—R3	R—K3
49	R—KB3	R—K5
50	R—R3	K—R3
51	R—R6	R—K4
52	K—R4	R—K5+
53	K—R3	R—K2
54	K—R4	R—K4
55	R—N6	K—N2
56	R—N4	K—R3
57	R—N6	R—K8
58	K—R3	R—R8+
59	K—N2	R—R8
60	K—R3	R—R5

Draw agreed! Five hours of play had elapsed at this point. The American had kept his lead intact for the third time: 9½:6½ in favour of Fischer!

17

Every game was different and the seventeenth was no exception. Experts began to enjoy, more than ever, the versatility of both rivals in the rich variety of their opening systems, and chess fans were happy for the publicity which this match gave to their beloved game.

Yet, the reporters remained worried. Throughout the world, millions of readers were following the chess news, but many of them for the first time. One could not entertain them just with a description of what happened on the chess board. If it were the shooting of a film, the recipe would be a simple one: the principal actor and actress, during the making of the film, find each other so wonderful that afterwards they cannot resist falling in love. Nothing of that kind of a story could be applied to the chess match. And the journalists were frightened that the number of Fischer's subjects for complaint — percentages, cameras, children, noise, back-stage room, rows of spectator's chairs — might soon be exhausted.

But there was nothing to worry about. A delightful misunderstanding arose between the two rival sides, outwardly adding spice to the quiet struggle on the board. Tired of several draws in a row, Fischer now felt that Spassky's strictly restrained and indifferent behaviour about anything that occurred around the chess table, could be an unfriendly gesture to the challenger who restlessly strove for "perfect conditions". At the same time, tired of Fischer's demands despite his constantly having the advantage in points, the Soviet side created a situation in which a mean psychological device had been invented by Fischer, to "unbalance" his opponent.

As uniformed policemen patrolled the playing hall to enforce silence, following a walkout threat by Fischer the same morning, a typewritten statement was issued in English and Russian, signed by the champion's second, grandmaster Efim Geller:

"The World Chess Championship Match now taking place in Reykjavik arouses a great interest in all parts of the world including the United States. Mr. B. Spassky, the other members of our delegation and I have been receiving many letters from various countries. A great number of the letters is devoted to an unknown in the chess history theme, i.e. a possibility to use non-chess means of influence on one of the participants.

"It is said that Mr. R. Fischer's numerous "whims", his claims to the organizers, his constant late arrivals for the games, his demands to play in the closed-door room, ungrounded protests, etc. have been deliberately aimed at exercizing pressure on the opponent, unbalancing Mr. B. Spassky and making him lose his fighting spirit.

"I consider that Mr. R. Fischer's behaviour runs counter to the Amsterdam Agreement which provides for gentlemanly behaviour of the participants. I believe that the arbiters have had enough facts to demand that Mr. R. Fischer should observe the provisions of the match in this respect. Furthermore it must be done immediately, now that the fight is approaching its decisive stage.

"We have received letters saying that some electronic devices and chemical substance which can be in the playing hall are being used to influence Mr. B. Spassky. The letters mention, in particular, Mr. R. Fischer's chair and the influence of the special lighting over the stage installed on the demand of the U.S. side.

"All this may seem fantastic, but some objective factors in this connection make us think of such seemingly fantastic suppositions.

"Why, for instance, does Mr. R. Fischer strongly protest against film-shooting even though he suffers financial losses? One of the reasons might be that he is anxious to get rid of the constant objective control over the behaviour and physical state of the participants. The same could be supposed if we take into consideration his repeated demands to conduct the games behind closed doors and to remove the spectators from the first seven rows.

"It is surprising that the Americans can be found in the playing hall when the games are not taking place, even at night. Mr. F. Cramer's demand that Mr. R. Fischer should be given "his" particular chair, though both the chairs look identical and are made by the same American firm.

"I would also like to note that having known Mr. B. Spassky for many years, it is the first time that I observe such unusual slackening of concentration and display of impulsiveness in his playing which I cannot account for by Mr. R. Fischer's exclusive impressive playing. On the contrary, in some games the Challenger made technical mistakes and in a number of games he did not grasp the position.

"In connection with the above said our delegation has handed over the statement to this effect to the Chief Arbiter and the Organizers of the Match which contains the urgent request that the playing hall and the things in it should be examined with the assistance of competent experts and that the possibility of the presence of any outsiders in the place allocated to the participants should be excluded.

E. Geller.
August 22, 1972"

The atmosphere of the match was, thanks to Fischer, strange enough already, but now, thanks to the Soviet statement, it was transformed into a James Bond style happening.

It was reported that Fischer laughed the statement off. His biographer, Frank Brady, remarked that it was the most contrived excuse for losing a game of chess ever heard, and that 'the Russians have accepted idle speculation'. "It is not all that unusual to want your own chair. It is like asking for your own bed. It is where your body fits."

A neutral observer, a young Rhodesian lawyer, was amazed: "Pathetic! It is just the thing I would expect Fischer to say." (The preceding year in Argentina, Fischer had hesitated to accept a ride in a private plane, saying: "Suppose the Russians did like something with the engine... People do not realize how they would like to get me out of the way.")

After the game, chief referee Lothar Schmid said that he would treat the Soviet demand "with all seriousness, as I have all American protests." He added that it sounded a little fantastic, 'but there was some truth in it, that Fischer's behaviour had not always been "gentlemanly", and that Fischer's aide had, on a number of occasions, interfered with the playing podium, altering the lighting and changing the champion's chiar.

The long-patient referee immediately responded to a Soviet objection that the player's area in the playing hall was open to outsiders. A 24-hour guard was posted at the hall and the backstage closed to everyone but the two players. The tournament building looked more impressive than ever with the increased crowd of elegant Icelandic policemen around it.

The game was equally exciting. Fischer played the Pirc Defence for the first time in his career, but Spassky made prompt answers and did not look surprized. He built an aggressive set-up, and Fischer entered early complications. Spassky gave up a pawn but had a terrible attack. Giving up an exchange Fischer got out of the worst of the trouble. The game was adjourned with material advantage to White but Black had very good drawing chances.

After Geller cited the challenger's habitual tardiness as one example of his unsporting behaviour, Schmid entreated his second, Rev. William Lombardy, to get him to the chess board on time. For the first time in the match, Fischer arrived punctually for the continuation of the 17th game. Greeted by pleased applause as he entered, Fischer looked unusually jaunty.

That was perhaps one of Spassky's last opportunities to shake Fischer's firm standing on a safe distance of three points, and a long fight for a full point was expected from Spassky. Instead, a repetition of the position followed, and Fischer was quick to claim a draw. The puzzle remained whether Spassky had not seen any possibility to play for win and agreed to the inevitable, or just forgot about the repetition (like Petrosian once did in a superior position against Fischer in Buenos Aires) and thus spoilt his chance. Anyhow, the novelty was that the champion once peered suspiciously up at the lighting before turning his attention back to the game.

White: Spassky
Black: Fischer
Pirc Defence

1 P—K4

This move has become a standard weapon of the title holder in the final stage of the match.

1 ...   P—Q3!

Fischer has never played like that before. According to his present tactics he does not use the same line twice in the match.

2 P—Q4   P—KN3

More flexible and sometimes more complicated than the straightforward 2 ... N-KB3 3 N-QB3 P-KN3.

3 N—QB3

Taking better control of the Q5 square and leaving thhe posssssibility of playing P-KB4 until later. White also has to take care of Black's counter in the centre (... P-QB4) and the developing move covers the diagonal K1-QR5 where the black queen (after an eventual ... P-QB4) could otherwise come with check.

3 ...   N—KB3

Coming back to the recognized continuation.

4 P—KB4

The most energetic attempt to control more space and the K5 square. The alternative 4 N-B3 is less sharp.

4 ...   B—N2

5 N—B3

This is the favourite method of Fischer himself, when playing White.

5 ...   P—B4

The usual continuation is 5 ... 0-0 6 B-Q3 N-B3, but it could hardly surprise Spassky. Therefore, Fischer chooses an unclear continuation, favoured by Benko, and less explored in the praxis.

6 PxP

Interesting, but probably premature is 6 P-K5 KN-Q2 7 B-B4 0-0 (crucial is 7 ... BPxP!) 8 P-K6 N-N3?! 9 PxP+ K-R1 10 P-KR4!! with a very strong attack (Velimirovic-Rajkovic, Skopje 1971).

The alternative 6 B-N5+ B-Q2 7 P-K5 N-N5 8 P-K6 (or 8 N-N5 BxB 9 QxN, Estrin-Shashin, USSR 1967) BxB 9 PxP+ K-Q2 10 NxB Q-R4+ 11 N-B3 PxP 12 NxP BxN 13 QxB N-B3 does not give White anything. Zuckerman-Benko, New York 1967.

6 ...   Q—R4

Necessary, for after 6 ... PxP 7 QxQ+ KxQ 8 P-K5 Black could not feel happy in such an endgame.

7 B—Q3

7 PxP? would be met by 7 ... NxP, and 7 Q-Q3 QxP 8 B-K3 Q-QR4 9 N-Q2 0-0! 10 N-N3 Q-R4 11 B-K2 B-N5 12 P-KR3 N-B3 would not worry Black either. Klovan-Vitolinsh, USSR 1971.

7 ...   QxBP
8 Q—K2   0—0
9 B—K3   Q—QR4

Playable is 9 ... Q-B2 10 0-0 QN-Q2 11 P-KR3 P-QR3 12 P-QR4 P-N3 13 Q-B2 B-N2 14 Q-R4 N-B4 (or 14 ... B-B3) 15 P-B5 P-QN4. Tal-Gufeld, USSR 1970.

10 0—0   B—N5!

Suggested by Fridstein in his book of the Pirc Defence. It looks more natural than the other moves:

1) 10 ... N-B3 11 P-KR3! B-Q2 12 P-QR3! KR-B1 13 Q-B2 B-K1 (or 13 ... P-K3 also with the inferior game. Velimirovic-Tringov, Skopje 1971) 14 P-B5! with pressure for White. Olafsson-Benko, Wijk aan Zee 1969;

2) 10 ... QN-Q2 11 P-KR3 (11 Q-K1!) P-QR3 12 Q-B2 P-K4 13 PxP PxP 14 Q-R4 P-QN4 15 B-KR6 B-N2 with chances for both sides. Ree-Benko, Wijk aan Zee 1967.

11 QR—Q1   N—B3
12 B—B4!

All of a sudden, with his peculiar skill, Spassky transforms his position into an aggressive set-up, putting the bishop on a strong diagonal. The ordinary alternative was 12 P-KR3.

12 ...   N—R4!

It was now Fischer's turn to show his ability to find a way for immediate counter-play. The position becomes very tricky and with chances for both sides. While attacking, White has to think of his queen side because of Black's threat ... KBxN.

13 B—N3

It was necessary to secure the bishop on its active diagonal. White offers a pawn, placing his hope in the weaknesses of Black's king side. The continuation 13 R-Q5 Q-B2 14 R-KN5!? could not work well after 14 ... N-B3, and the rook would be rather displaced.

13 ...   KBxN

Accepting the challenge. As a matter of fact, it was the only logical chance to keep some counterplay, before White increased his pressure even more.

14 PxB   QxBP
15 P—B5!

This move opens the diagonals and files towards the sensitive position of Black's king which no longer has the protection of his good black-squared bishop.

15 ...   N—B3!

It is the natural consequence of Black's 13th move, reestablishing the previous centralized position of his pieces, covering the KB-file, attacking White's king pawn and threatening also to bring the queen to K4.

The alternative was 15 ... N-K4 and if 16 B-Q4? (correct is 16 PxP RPxP 17 Q-B2) 16 ... N-KB5, but not 15 ... PxP 16 PxP BxP and White would have several attractive ways to continue his attack against the insufficiently protected black king.

16   P—KR3
White could not activate his pieces without getting rid of the pin.

16   ...   BxN
17   QxB
Defends the king pawn for a while and, more important, seeks to bring White's queen closer to the opponent's king. One possible manoeuvre could be Q-B4-R6.

17   ...   N—QR4
Black defends very cleverly in a dangerous position, wanting to get rid of one of the very unpleasant white bishops. 17 ... N-K4 would be wrong because of 18 Q-B4, and 17 ... Q-K4 just the same, because of 18 B-Q5!

18   R—Q3   Q—B2
Not 18 ... Q-K4 because of 19 B-Q5 and the black queen would be in trouble.

19   B—R6
The best choice now is to go for material gain, as 19 B-Q5 was not clear. The continuation in the game offers White the chance of correcting the pawn structure on his queen side.

19   ...   NxB
20   BPxN   Q—B4+
21   K—R1?
Automatically played. Correct was 21 R-K3 and if 21 ... KR-B1 22 P-KN4 saving a tempo in the attack.

21   ...   Q—K4?!
Black remains faithful to his concept of giving up an exchange for a very solid position and some positional compensation. But, after White's 21st move, Black could well play 21 ... KR-B1 22 PxP BPxP 23 P-KN4 (23 R-Q5 Q-B6) Q-K4 attacking White's KP.

22   BxR   RxB
23   R—K3
This is that loss of a tempo mentioned at move 21, but now, with an exchange up, it is still in time.

23   ...   R—B1
It is essential for Black to be able to take the open QB-file just in time. White's chances to win are now very small.

24   PxP
Perhaps 24 Q-B4 was better, not being afraid of 24 ... QxQ 25 RxQ P-KN4 26 R-B2.

24   ...   RPxP
25   Q—B4
Black's queen is too strong in the centre, and White has no better choice than to enter the endgame.

25   ...   QxQ
26   RxQ   N—Q2
Preventing 27 P-K5 and an unfavourable opening of files for Black.

27   R—B2   N—K4
28   K—R2   R—B8!
29   R(3)—K2   N—B3
Closing the file to White's rooks.

30   R—B2   R—K8
Black has to keep his active rook on the board and thus keep White's rooks busy with the defence of his weak pawns.

31	R(KB)—K2	R—QR8
32	K—N3	K—N2
33	R(B)—Q2	R—KB8
34	R—KB2	R—K8
38	R(B)—K2	R—KB8
36	R—K3	

White does not wish a draw by repetition of moves.

36	...	P—R3
37	R—QB3	R—K8
38	R—B4	

White has slightly improved the position of his rook on B4, but, with three islands of white pawns, it is difficult to activate the white pieces sufficiently. 38 ... N-K4 would be bad because of 39 R-B7.

38	...	R—KB8
39	R(2)—QB2	R—QR8
40	R—B2	R—K8

The game was adjourned and White sealed the 41st move.

41 R(2)—B2

An interesting idea was also 41 R-N2 intending, with P-QN4-N5, to open the QN-file for a rook and try to penetrate with the heavy pieces on the seventh rank.

41 ... P—KN4!

This looks a little mysterious and surprising, but it is a natural move which captures space and, after an eventual White sacrifice on QB6, would make Black's central passed pawns more effective. The other reason for the move in the game however, is to free the square KN3 for the knight. Also, after 42 R-N2 R-QR8 43 P-N4 K-B3 44 P-N5 PxP 45 RxP RxP 46 RxQNP N-K4 47 R(4)-B7 N-N3 it would be quite obvious why Black's 41st move is useful.

42	R—B1	R—K7
43	R(1)—B2	R—K8
44	R—B1	R—K7
45	R(1)—B2	

Draw. Black announced that he can create the identical position with his 41st, 43rd and 45th moves by playing 45 ... R-K8. The score 10:7 to Fischer.

18

Before the seventeenth game, Fischer threatened to quit the championship unless immediate steps were taken to improve "worsening" conditions in the 2500-seat auditorium. "I shall consider the match summarily terminated and there will be no further play under any conditions" — were Fischer's warning words in his letter to Schmid. An accompanying letter from Fred Cramer said that Sunday's (16th) game had been as noisy as "a ball game in Milwaukee" (this is where Fischer's spokesman lived).

Schmid called a meeting (one among many) of American and Icelandic officials. After two hours of talks, the Icelandic Chess Federation agreed to bow saying that conditions in the hall were "normal, even good". The referee then suggested to Fischer that he seek a two-day medical postponement, buying time for talks, but Cramer said that the challenger had "never felt better in his life".

Schmid called a meeting (one among many of American and Icelandic officials.) After two hours of talks, the Icelandic Chess Federation agreed to bow to Fischer's condition for playing on stage and gouged out a semi-circle of seats at the front of the auditorium. There was now about thirty metres distance to the player's chess table, but the remaining rows were squeezed together to keep capacity seating. The organizers, already without film profits, were reluctant to suffer further financial loss.

Since long ago, the event in Reykjavik had consisted of two parts: the great match on the chess board and the great performance outside of it. Spassky had his share in the first part, but had almost nothing to do with the second one. That way, all headlines and attention went to Fischer and his constant demands, while the champion remained in the shadow and was in danger of getting an inferiority complex. The sensational Soviet press statement aimed at changing all that. A group of Icelandic scientists started their search by smear-testing the two chairs, to determine whether poison could have entered the champion's body that way, as one of the suggested Soviet hypotheses for Spassky's "unusual slackening of concentration and display of impulsiveness". The experts dismantled the 105 glass plates of the huge lighting canopy over the stage and came up with two dead flies. They took photographs for comparison with pre-match shots. Finally, they made 18 x-rays of each chair in case some devilish device had been embedded in the chrome or leather.

To Fischer's ultimatum of the previous day, Spassky's second Geller added his first official letter to Lothar Schmid. It was short, saying that the Soviet side was not consulted about the removal of the front rows of spectator's seats and protested against alterations in the seating arrangements.

Referee Schmid had a very busy day, being now obliged to answer protests from two sides. The Soviets were right in their claim and, while Fischer was sleeping as usual by day and could not be contacted, the front rows of seats were put back in place. The same afternoon the organizers compromised, trying not to fill these with newcomers until there would be no other choice.

Fortunately, Fischer did not want to pay attention to the outlook of the audience. The same evening Schmid was relieved to hear from Fischer the praise that "conditions were improving". "He asked me only during the game to remove someone he thought was snoring. But I could not find him. It is not so easy to find the right man," added the happy referee. However, Schmid felt tired before dinner and complained, as usual, of having "pains in stomach".

After Geller's description of Fischer's habitual tardiness as being "ungentle-manly", the challenger managed one prompt arrival for the continuation of the 17th game, and then backslided to his normal way of life. Fischer arrived eight minutes late for the game, which this time he opened with his favourite king pawn. It could mean that he had become tired of the levelled fight in the second half of the match, and wanted a quick decision.

Being three points behind, Spassky was tired of a slow progress too, and was less cautious with Black than ever. The eighteenth game was a hard struggle, with plenty of tricky manoeuvring and chances for both sides. Spassky lost patience first and opened the position to his disadvantage. "Now, we can pack home" — said a journalist. (He had stayed in Iceland for two months by then.)

But, Fischer played fast and somewhere missed his way. Spassky immediately recovered, made the best moves and after the adjournment the experts realized with astonishment that the picture had changed abruptly and Black was not worse. Next day, after some hesitation by Fischer, the moves were quickly repeated, the most convenient way to make a draw in this match and thus escape the necessity of "humiliating offers".

White: Fischer
Black: Spassky
Sicilian Defence
   1   P—K4
Both players took it for the best weapon, at last.
   1   ...   P—QB4
This did not mean any peaceful mood.
   2   N—KB3   P—Q3
   3   N—B3   N—QB3
   4   P—Q4   PxP
   5   NxP   N—B3
   6   B—KN5!
The first Rauzer Attack in Fischer's career.

Never repeat the same line was Fischer's rule in this match. Now, it meant for-saking his favourite Sozin line with 6 B-QB4 as played in the fourth game of the match.
   6   ...   P—K3
   7   Q—Q2   P—QR3

Popular, but a more modest line is 7 ... B-K2 8 0-0-0 0-0.
   8   0—0—0   B—Q2
Because of the threat N(4)-N5, Black's 7th move was the necessary preparation of this move, which goes for faster counter-play on the queen side.
   9   P—B4   B—K2
   10 N—B3
Threatening 11 P-K5. The interesting alternative is 10 Q-K2, or 10 P-B5 R-QB1 11 PxP PxP 12 B-QB4 NxN 13 QxN Q-R4 14 BxN PxB 15 B-N3 with the better game. Holmov-Taimanov, Leningrad 1967.
   10 ...   P—N4
   11 BxN
11 P-K5 P-N5! 12 PxN (unclear is 12 PxP?! PxN 13 QxP B-KB1 14 P-B5 Q-R4 15 BxN PxB 16 PxP PxP 17 QxP R-KN1 18 B-B4 B-N2. Burger-Mednis, USA 1970) 12 ... PxN 13 QxBP PxP 14 B-R4 P-QR4 (14 ... P-Q4 15 K-N1 N-N5?! 16 N-Q4 R-

QB1 17 Q-QN3! Q-R4 18 B-K1 B-R5 19 Q-QR3! is winning for White. Matanovic-Jansa, Lugano Olympiad 1968) 15 K-N1 N-N5 16 P-QR3 R-QB1 17 Q-Q2 N-Q4 18 P-B4 N-N3 gives counterplay to Black. Jimenez-Taimanov, Havana 1967.

11 ...   PxB

Interesting but unclear is the pawn sacrifice 11 ... BxB!? (in order not to spoil his pawn structure) 12 QxP B-K2 (weaker is 12 ... P-N5 13 N-QR4 R-R2 14 Q-B5! Q-N1 15 Q-K3 with better chances. S. Garcia-Polugaevsky, Havana 1967) 13 Q-Q2 P-N5 14 N-K2 R-R2 15 N(2)-Q4 Q-N3 16 NxN BxN 17 B-Q3 0-0 18 N-K5 B-QN4 19 K-N1 R-B1. Schmid-R. Byrne, San Juan 1969.

12 B—Q3!

This normal, developing move is Fischer's novelty! It deviates from previous tournament games, where 12 P-B5 (with the idea of developing White's king bishop to R3) was played:

1) 12 ... Q-R4 13 K-N1 0-0-0 (or 13 ... P-R4 14 P-KN3 N-K4 15 NxN BPxN 16 B-R3! with the advantage, Vasjukov-Partos, Bucharest 1967) 14 P-KN3 K-N1 15 B-R3 B-QB1 (or 15 ... R-QB1 16 PxP BxP [16 ... PxP 17 N-Q5!] 17 B-B5 R-B2 18 N-Q5 with a positional advantage, Bihovski-Averbah, USSR 1967) 16 KR-K1 P-R4 17 Q-K3 B-Q2 18 N-K2 N-K4 19 N-B4 with pressure for White. Tal-R. Byrne, Havana Olympiad 1966;

2) 12 ... Q-N3! 13 K-N1 0-0-0 14 P-KN3 K-N1 15 B-R3 P-N5 16 N-K2 P-K4 17 P-B4 N-R4! 18 P-N3 B-B3! 19 Q-Q3 N-N2 20 N-Q2 B-B1 21 Q-KB3 B-R3 22 KR-K1 draw. Boleslavsky-Taimanov, USSR 1970.

12 ...   Q—R4

13 K—N1   P—N5
14 N—K2   Q—QB4

Activating the queen and leaving the road free to Black's QRP.

15 P—B5

The standard method to exercize pressure on Black's weakened pawn formation in the centre.

15 ...   P—QR4

Black's counter-chance is to increase the pressure on the queen side, where he has more space.

16 N—B4   P—R5

Both players develop their initiative in their respective areas of the board. Black has a bishop pair, but also problems because of the sensitive pawn formation in the centre and an eventual obligation to keep his king there.

17 R—QB1

Preparing to meet Black's attack with an attempt to open the QB-file by P-B3, and thus obtain more air on the queen side.

17 ...   R—QN1

After 17 ... P-R6 18 P-QN3 Q-B6 (otherwise 19 P-B3) 19 QxQ PxQ 20 B-B4 Black would stand worse.

18 P—B3   P—N6

Opening the QB-file would be to White's favour.

19 P—QR3

This way White avoids the attack on his king and has free hands elsewhere, but he remains cramped on the queen side.

19 ...   N—K4

Using the possibility to diminish the pressure of White's pieces on the black KP, which cannot move (19 ... P-K4? 20 N-Q5).

20 KR—B1

Bringing a new piece into play after a long reflection. 20 NxN BPxN would increase the power of Black's bishops and central pawns, and 20 N-Q4 NxB would produce something similar to the continuation in the game.

20 ... N—B5

21 BxN

Otherwise White would have to count on a knight sacrifice on R6, and Black would have dangerous passed pawns in front of his opponent's king. Now Black's queen will be a very strong piece on its new square.

21 ... QxB

22 R(QB)—K1

Played quickly. After 22 KR-K1 White would be better able to control the central files (22 ... PxP? 23 N-Q4!), but the move in the game has another idea — pressure along the KB-file.

22 ... K—Q1!

Finding the only safe way to connect his rooks and remove his king from the K-file. The alternative 22 ... P-K4 23 N-Q5 B-B3 24 R-K3 BxN 25 QxB QxQ 26 PxQ would favour White (because of the manoeuvre N-Q2-K4).

23 K—R1

Removing the king from the QN1-KB5 diagonal.

23 ... R—N4

24 N—Q4 R—R4

25 N—Q3

Intending to go to QN4 and meeting the threat of ... P-K4. Both sides now have chances.

25 ... K—B2

26 N—N4

Both sides have improved the positions of their pieces.

26 ... P—R4

Now that White has consolidated his control of the central squares, Black had to meet the threat 27 Q-R6.

27 P—N3

Keeping the tension.

27 ... R—K4

28 N—Q3 R—QN1!?

Black does not try to offer the repetition of moves with 28 ... R-R4. Instead he offers the exchange.

29 Q—K2

Aiming at the strong black queen. After 29 PxP PxP 30 NxR QPxN 31 N-B3 Black would have counterplay with his activated bishop pair (31 ... B-N4!).

29 ... R—R4

30 PxP PxP

31 R—B2

Removing the rook from the KB1-QR6 diagonal. The position is unclear and Black has good possibilities. But now he loses patience.

31 ... P—K4

This move is satisfactory although 31 ... K-N2 was also playable as a preparation for the break in the centre. 31 ... P-Q4 would be met by 32 P-K5.

32 N—KB5 BxN

33 RxB P—Q4

On this move Black put his hopes — in vain.

34 PxP QxQP?

Only now, probably, Black realized that he could not play 34 ... RxP and have active counterplay because of the tactical blow 35

N-B4 (35 ... QxQ? 36 NxR+) winning material. Yet the move in the game was a mistake and the correct continuation was 34 ... R-Q1! 35 N-B4 QxQ 36 RxQ K-Q3! (36 ... PxN? 37 RxB+) 37 NxP RxP 38 R-K1 K-K3 39 R(5)-B1 R-Q7 and Black can have a draw whenever he wants.

35   N—N4

White plays fast on impulse. An interesting possibility was 35 N-B4! (to prevent Black's heavy pieces occupying the Q-file) 35 ... Q-B2 (otherwise White's queen may check on B4) 36 RxRP threatening 37 Q-K4 and an irresistible attack would follow.

35   ...   Q—Q2

Not 35 ... BxN immediately because of 36 BPxB and White captures the open files first. 35 ... Q-K3 36 R-B4! would bring White's rook quickly into attack.

36   RxRP

Capturing a pawn but taking the rook away from the central files. Therefore, more effective was 36 R-B3! BxN 37 BPxB and Black would have more problems to safeguard his king.

36   ...   BxN!
37   BPxP   R—Q4

Black can feel better now. He has a central file and his king has escaped.

38   R—B1+   K—N2

There is not other place to go: 38 ... K-Q1 39 R-R8+ or 38 ... K-N3 39 Q-B2+.

39   Q—K4   R—QB1!

Getting rapidly out of trouble, thanks to his mating threats on the eighth rank.

40   R—QN1

An unfortunate necessity because of the poorly protected first rank.

40   ...   K—N3
41   R—R7   R—Q5!

An excellent intermediate move which chases White's queen from its dominant position in the centre.

42   Q—N6

White's king is too passive for the endgame, and therefore he prefers to keep the queens on the board. The game was adjourned here and Black sealed his move.

42   ...   Q—B3

Obvious and good, keeping the king well covered.

43   R—KB7

In case of 43 Q-N7 R-B2 Black would feel safe in the endgame because of his more active king.

43   ...   R—Q3
44   Q—R6

44 P-KR4 Q-B7 brings nothing to White.

44   ...   Q—KB6

Preventing 45 Q-K3+.

45   Q—R7   Q—B3

Back to safety. The threat is 46 ... R-B2, in order to exchange those white pieces which are active.

46   Q—R6   Q—KB6
47   Q—R7   Q—B3

Draw. The score: 10½:7½ in favour of Fischer.

19

Throughout the day preceeding the nineteenth game, Fischer was in seclusion, observing the Sabbath of his world-wide Church of God and his aide said that in mid-afternoon he was asleep. Richard Stein served the legal papers (in the suit bought by movie maker Chester Fox) on Fischer's personal representative, Fred Cramer, as Cramer crossed his hotel lobby. "Do you think that we would wake him up for that!" he said. (The suit was for $1,750,000.)

Fox had no written agreement (who had?) with Fischer, whose objections prevented filming except in the first and eighth games. But, Chester Fox contends that Fischer exclusively had destroyed a potentially lucrative contract with the Icelandic Chess Federation, granting the American exclusive movie rights. The suit required Fischer or a representative to appear within twenty days before Judge Constance Baker Motley in a New York City court. It was part of a triple-barrelled legal assault, planned by Stein, to tie up Fischer's assets in the U.S.A., Iceland and Britain, pending settlement of Fischer's differences with Fox. "We are getting near the end and I do not want to see that money wind up in a Swiss bank" Stein said.

After conferences with officials of the Icelandic Chess Federation which went on throughout the day, Stein said that he had agreed not to file a suit under Icelandic law. In return the Icelandic Federation ("They are such good, honest people" said the enchanted attorney), yielded to Fox its claim for 20% of any eventual profit from filming the match. The president of the Icelandic Federation, Gudmundur Thorarinsson, told newspapermen: "We did not want to end this match of the century with a fiasco, handing over empty envelopes to the players with a lawsuit over their heads."

"Fox remained hopeful of filming the remaining games," said Stein. Thorarinsson admitted that the Icelandic Federation faced losses of more than five million kronur (about $60,000) so far. If the Icelandic prize fund of $125,000 remained safe, the British half was not affected by this agreement. Attorney Stein thought that he would go to Britain next week for a possible suit to freeze the £50,000 contributed to the prize fund by British financier James Slater. According to Stein the case could take anything from three to five years. This did not seem to impress Fischer sufficiently to make him change his ideas about the film cameras.

In the latest off the board fighting, the American camp again demanded that the front rows of the 2,500 seat playing hall be kept empty to protect Fischer who cannot stand noise when he is thinking. The match organizers, having an interest in this matter, but openly supporting the Russian side, rejected the demand. As it happened, an unusually warm and sunny day (the only one in a long time) lured the Icelanders outdoors. Even many chess buffs were away from the hall. The expected overflow crowd on Sunday did not show up. It was therefore possible that the front row of seats be kept in place (for the sake of Spassky), but empty (for the sake of Fischer), who restricted himself to only one personal complaint about the noise after the thirteenth move, and everything went normally according to the accepted routine of other chess competitions.

There were almost no problems concerning Fischer at that moment, only with his representative. Schmid wrote a stinging "Dear Fred" letter in a reply to Cramer and his allegations of favouritism towards Spassky. Schmid said that Cramer's letter was largely inaccurate in content and that the American had erred in signing it as an official of F.I.D.E. (Cramer is a vice president) instead of as Fischer's personal representative. The referee wrote of "The absolute necessity of making my own decision without any interference from outside sources". Schmid also told Cramer that he wouldn't attempt to tell Cramer his job "just as it is not for you to have the right to give me official advice."

Cramer was arguing that he wanted to have Schmid treat Fischer as fairly as the Russians. It looked as though the "Cramer-Schmid show", as it was jokingly called by the referee because of their almost daily correspondence, was going to leave a bitter taste.

The Soviet suspicion about the possible use of electronic devices and chemical methods on Spassky, was followed by a scientific search which disclosed nothing. On Sunday afternoon the two players, according to the newspapers, shook hands cordially. Spassky, in a suit and waistcoat, left the stage after making his first move. Fischer, in a new blue-white suit, was only two minutes late — exceptionally punctual for him. As was his habit, Spassky then returned to the board and they settled down to play.

After his bitter experiences with the 1 P-Q4 in the first half of the match, Spassky turned to his favourite 1 P-K4, and for good. If nothing else he was giving his opponent more trouble with 1 P-K4. The game was an Alekhine Defence this time, the one with which Fischer had scored a success in the thirteenth game. Of course, Fischer never repeats the same line in this match, and he therefore deviated at an early stage of the game. But Spassky was not taken aback and soon he captured the initiative.

When bishops of opposite colour appeared on the board there were expert predictions that it would be "a dull game". Only a few moves later however, Spassky offered a piece sacrifice. "It's getting exciting" said Fischer's second, grandmaster Bill Lombardy. The title holder felt, nevertheless, that the time was right. He was hoping for an irresistable attack, which one or two moves later had vanished. The champion couldn't hide his disgust and bit a curve on his lip while he was pouring coffee during Fischer's absence from the board. Fischer, in contrast, felt relaxed, and was hurrying busily around looking for his own supply of drinks and food behind the stage.

The sixth draw in a row looked inevitable and with it the burial of Spassky's last hopes to change the course of destiny. The Russian was still three points behind and would have the White pieces only twice more even if the match went to its limit.

White: Spassky
Black: Fischer
Alekhine's Defence

1	P—K4	N—KB3
2	P—K5	N—Q4
3	P—Q4	P—Q3
4	N—KB3	

Sooner or later one could have expected that Fischer would again reply with this defence with which he triumphed in the thirteenth game of the match.

The sharpest line is 4 P-QB4 N-N3 5 P-B4, but Spassky obviously doesn't mind once more entering the line played in the thirteenth game, but being better ready to meet it this time.

4	...	B—N5!

Fischer's normal tactics, not repeating the same line twice. In the thirteenth game he replied 4 ... P-KN3.

5	B—K2	P—K3

This appears to be more flexible than 5 ... N-QB3 e.g. 6 PxP BPxP 7 0-0 P-K3 8 P-KR3 B-R4 9 P-B4 N-N3 10 QN-Q2! B-K2 11 P-QN3 0-0 12 B-N2 P-Q4 13 P-B5 N-Q2 14 P-R3 B-B3 15 P-QN4 P-QR3 16 R-K1 R-K1 17 Q-N3! and White has the better game because of his good control of the K5 square. Matulovic-Janosevic, Yugoslavia 1970.

6	0—0	B—K2
7	P—KR3	

Deviating slightly from previous games: 7 P-B4 N-N3 8 N-B3 0-0 (if 8 ... N(N1)-Q2 9 PxP PxP 10 P-QN3 0-0 11 P-KR3 B-R4 12 P-QR4 N-B3 13 P-R5 N-Q2 14 P-R6 P-QN3 15 B-R3 P-Q4 16 R-K1; or 8 ... N-B3 9 PxP PxP 10 P-Q5 PxP[10 ... N-R4 11 PxP BxP 12 N-Q5!] 11 PxP BxN 12 PxB! when

White has the advantage) 9 B-K3 N-B3 10 PxP PxP 11 P-Q5 PxP 12 NxP NxN 13 QxN Q-B2 14 QR-Q1! also gives White the advantage. Gipslis-Marovic, USSR-Yugoslavia match, Erevan 1971.

The move in the game seeks to interpolate P-KR3 without loss of time.

7	...	B—R4
8	P—B4	N—N3
9	N—B3	0—0
10	B—K3	P—Q4!?

Black does not choose to enter the continuation 10 ... N-B3 11 PxP PxP because of 12 P-Q5! with advantage to White.

The move played by Fischer was tried in the second and fourth games of the match for the ladies world championship between Nona Gaprindashvili and Alla Kushnir, Tiflis 1969. The idea is to build a pawn formation similar to that in the French Defence but with the favourable difference that Black's QB is actively developed. But here White also has some positional advantage in comparison with the French Defence. He has more space on the queen side thanks to the activated QBP.

11	P—B5	

11 P-QN3 looks playable, the idea being to deprive Black's knight of squares and to retain the tension in the centre with his pawns.

11	...	BxN

It is useful to destroy White's knight which controls the important squares Q4 and K5. Black should not play 11 ... N-B5 because of 12 BxN PxB 13 Q-K2 capturing the pawn.

12	BxB	

A drawish continuation would be 12 PxN BxB 13 PxBP BxQ 14 PxQ(Q) RxQ 15 KRxB, but White cannot be satisfied with any line of that kind. The ladies world champion Gaprindashvili tried in one game (with the moves P-KR3 B-R4 interpolated) the dubious PxB?! for White.

12	...	N—B5

Alla Kushnir played the more passive 12 ... N-B1.

13	P—QN3!	

The only way to keep the initiative. 13 B-B1 P-KN3 would slow down White's development and give excellent chances to his opponent.

| 13 | ... | NxB |
| 14 | PxN | P—QN3!? |

In spite of bishops of opposite colours, White has some advantage in development and space. Therefore this move might be overreaching a little.

15 P—K4!

Forcing Black to take a more passive attitude on the queen side. The opening of the position was to White's favour for he is better developed.

| 15 | ... | P—QB3 |

Black is obliged to close the long diagonal.

16 P—QN4

16 KPxP BPxP 17 P-QN4 N-B3 gives Black favourable development on the queen side.

| 16 | ... | NPxP |
| 17 | NPxP | Q—R4 |

A sharp move. Fischer is faithful to his enterprising style and doesn't like the passive continuation 17 ... N-Q2 because of 18 Q-R4, although 18 ... Q-B2 would still be playable and somehow safer. For instance 19 PxP KPxP 20 NxP PxN 21 BxP QR-Q1 and Black has disposed of the knight sacrifice on his Q4 and all associated threats.

18 NxP!?

This looks impressive but perhaps 18 Q-K1 was more efficient, keeping the threat against Black's Q4 outpost. True, in case of 18 ... B-N4 19 PxP BPxP 20 NxP QxQ 21 QRxQ PxN 22 BxP N-R3! 23 RxP RxR 24 BxQR K-B1 White would have nothing clear in his favour.

| 18 | ... | B—N4! |

Played instantly and showing that Black had been expecting White's sacrifice. White has no retreat for his knight and a queer situation has arisen with many tactical possibilities for both sides. With 18 ... KPxN Black would be looking for trouble: 19 PxP PxP 20 BxP N-Q2 21 RxP!

19 B—R5!?

Spending a move to force Black into accepting the sacrifice. If 19 Q-N3 or 19 Q-Q3 Black would have excellent counterplay after 19 ... N-R3! (but not 19 ... R-Q1 20 B-R5 P-N3 21 Q-KB3 or 19 ... KPxN 20 PxP N-Q2 21 PxP NxKP 22 PxN QxP+ 23 K-R1 QxKP 24 B-Q5 and White would have the better game for a long time).

| 19 | ... | BPxN! |

Freeing the square QB3 for Black's knight. Not 19 ... P-N3 20 N-B6+ BxN 21 PxB with an irresistible attack.

20 BxP+

20 RxP would be followed simply by 20 ... N-B3.

| 20 | ... | RxB |

Gaining a tempo for the counteraction.

21 RxR

Black cannot answer 21 ... KxR because of 22 Q-R5+.

| 21 | ... | Q—Q7! |

Killing the attack for White because the hanging White QP makes it impossible for White to keep the queens on. It shows that White has spoilt his chances with his 19th move. White could have played for more than a draw after 21 ... N-B3.

| 22 | QxQ | BxQ |
| 23 | QR—KB1 | N—B3 |

The moves for both sides are obvious now.

24	PxP	PxP
25	R—Q7	B—K6+
26	K—R1	BxP
27	P—K6	B—K4

It is safer to take the square Q6 from White's rook than to play the continuation 27 ... R-K1 28 R-Q6 N-K2 29 R-B1. Not 27 ... BxP? 28 R-QB7.

28   RxQP

28	...	R—K1
29	R—K1	RxP
30	R—Q6	K—B2

Dubious would be 30 ... RxR 31 PxR K-B2 31 R-B1! After the move in the game Black enters a drawish rook endgame. The pawn up has no value for White because of the active black king.

31	RxN	RxR
32	RxB	K—B3
33	R—Q5	K—K3
34	R—R5	P—KR3
35	K—R2	R—R3
36	P—B6	RxBP

Not 36 ... RxRP? 37 R-QB5! or 36 ... K-Q3 37 R-KB5 with the threat of 38 R-B7. As usual, the players are dragging out the dull ending to the time control.

37	R—QR5	P—R3
38	K—N3	K—B3
39	K—B3	R—B6+
40	K—B2	R—B7+

Draw agreed.

The score: 11:8 in favour of Fischer!

20

The match was obviously close to its end. There was no news. In other words, there were no protests on the eve of the twentieth game.

Yet, the game of chess, thanks to Fischer, will never again be the same. Still remembering last year, when a few thousand dollars was a very good prize in the best international competitions, it happened that the offer of Las Vegas to have another Fischer match there next year, for a prize fund of one million dollars, was a well founded rumour.

Fischer's lawyer, Paul Marshall, arrived from New York once more, telling that he had many offers for Bobby for one night appearances as a show business personality, and none of those offers was smaller than a six-fugure sum. What should Bobby do for not less than 100,000 dollars each time? Nothing special — play a few games in front of his audience or just talk a little on each evening, was the answer.

Yes, the match was nearing its end, for the President of F.I.D.E., Dr. Max Euwe, arrived in Reykjavik to attend the final ceremony, and the third member of Spassky's team, master Ivo Ney, left on the same day for the Soviet Union because of the beginning of the school season. While Spassky's entourage was diminishing in number, Fischer's was increasing. His friend, Argentinian master Quinteros arrived from Buenos Aires, and Bobby gave him his house to stay in, while he — the future champion — preferred his hotel now. On the other hand, Spassky began to live most of the time with his wife Larissa in a small house in the town, and enjoyed the domestic atmosphere more.

A study made on behalf of the Ministry of Finince revealed that the prize money to be awarded in the world chess championship match between Boris Spassky and Robert Fischer was subject to Government income tax and local income tax.

In view of the special nature of this prize money, the Government of Iceland decided to enact special legislation during the following session of the Icelandic Parliament to authorize exemption from taxation of the prize money and local authorities, for their part, agreed to that. "The decision not to levy tax on prize money is being made in the faith that it will not be subject to taxation in the contestants home countries," said the official statement on the day of the twentieth game.

For some time, from the fourteenth game on, Fischer had little success in reaching an initiative. Spassky was imposing his choice of lines and the leader in the match could not find anything substantial against them. A similar thing happened in this game. Fischer, in the end, hastened to enter a drawish ending, but Spassky twice avoided repeating moves. He squeezed some positional advantage till the adjournment but that was all. The continuation was no more than a sheer formality.

White: Fischer
Black: Spassky
Sicilian Defence

1 P—K4

Both players confessed only at the end of the match that they liked this move best.

1 ... P—QB4

Black wants a sharp fight too.

2 N—KB3 N—QB3

A more straightforward way to play the line than 2 ... P-Q3 as in earlier Spassky games. Was he afraid of the drawish 3 B-N5+?

3 P—Q4 PxP
4 NxP N—B3
5 N—QB3 P—Q3
6 B—KN5

No return to the Sozin! The move repeats the Rauzer line played in the eighteenth game.

6 ... P—K3
7 Q—Q2 P—QR3
8 0—0—0 B—Q2
9 P—B4 B—K2

Black is ready to follow the footsteps of the eighteenth game too, but ...

10 B—K2

This looks like a brand new move, but has been played before in a few games, first by Darga in 1964, then by Kavalek in 1967 and also in Robert Byrne versus Mednis in the United States Championship. The challenger obviously was not pleased with anything that chess theory could offer White and had to find something that is missing from the books, even if it looks like a normal developing move.

In the eighteenth game Fischer replied with the most frequent continuation, 10 N-

B3 but couldn't have been pleased with the result. 10 P-B5 would have been another rather unsuccessful choice from tournament practice.

10 ... 0—0

Premature would be 10 ... P-R3 11 B-R4 NxP 12 N(3)xN BxB 13 NxP+. Instead of going for queen side action with P-QN4 Black changes his mind and castles short. This could remind players of the other line with 7 ... B-K2 8 0-0-0 0-0 9 P-B4, but there is no similar example for, in that order of moves 9 ... P-QR3 would come too late because of 10 BxN BxB 11 NxN PxN 12 QxP.

In the game Kavalek-Brasket, Chicago 1968, 10 ... Q-B2 11 B-B3 QR-B1 was played. After Spassky's move, White is faced with an important decision — what kind of plan shall he adopt in this new version of the Rauzer line?

11 B—B3

Improving the activity of the bishop and controlling the centre better, making it more difficult for Black to play P-QN4. This eleventh move is the logical consequence of his tenth.

11 ... P—R3

In the game Kavalek-Barden 1969, 11 ... R-B1 was played first and then 12 K R-K1 P-R3 13 B-R4 NxP and White was in some trouble.

12 B—R4

An unclear alternative would be 12 P-KR4, but White doesn't look for such things just now. 12 BxN BxB 13 NxN QBxN 14 QxP BxN would offer nothing to White.

12 ... NxP!

Going for simplifications of a known kind.

13 BxB

13 N(3)xN BxB 14 NxP was playable too.

13 ...   NxQ

Otherwise, Black would remain a piece down.

14 BxQ   N(7)xB

Forced again in order to keep the material balance. 14 ... NxN 15 B-K7! would be a dangerous adventure for Black.

15 NxN(KB3)   KRxB

16 RxP

It begins to look like a drawish ending. This should not disturb White.

16 ...   K—B1

16 ... B-K1 was simple too but Black wishes to keep more pieces on the board.

17 KR—Q1

Preventing Black from escaping the exchanges.

17 ...   K—K2

18 N—QR4

Developing activity of his own but Black can protect the dark squares rather easily.

18 ...   B—K1

19 RxR   RxR

20 N—B5

Looking for a little bit more, for 20 RxR could not worry Black with his king near the queen side.

20 ...   R—N1

Using the opportunity to look for a more complex fight in the endgame. 20 ... RxR+ 21 KxR N-Q1 would suffice only for a draw.

21 R—Q3

With the intention to 'punish' his ambitious opponent and give more meaning to the position of White's knight on QB5.

21 ...   P—QR4

Removing the pawn from the attacked square in order to make his QN pawn movable.

22 R—N3   P—QN4

Black didn't like the drawish possibility 22 ... P-QN3 23 N-R6 R-N2 24 N-B5.

23 P—QR3

23 R-B3 would be met by the unpleasant 23 ... N-N5 threatening 24 ... NxRP+.

23 ...   P—R5

Black doesn't mind a certain weakening

of his dark squares, because his advanced pawns make White's pawn majority rather ineffective.

24 R—B3   R—Q1

25 N—Q3   P—B3

26 R—B5   R—N1

27 R—B3   P—N4

As at the 22nd move, Black is not pleased to offer a repetition of moves by 27 ... R-Q1 but tries to make his pawn majority in the king side more valuable.

28 P—KN3

Not letting the mass of black pawns become powerful.

28 ...   K—Q3

29 N—B5   P—KN5

Another search for activity which has the drawback of consolidating the opponent's control of the black squares.

30 N—K4+   K—K2

31 N—K1   R—Q1

32 N—Q3

If 32 ... N-Q5 33 R-B7+ R-Q2 34 R-B8 White would have the threat 35 NxP.

32 ...   R—Q5

33 N(4)—B2   P—R4

34 R—B5   R—Q4

White's rook is too active. Black is looking for a minor piece endgame where he has more space.

35 R—B3

After 35 RxR PxR Black's pieces would be more active but it could not be of decisive effect.

35 ...   N—Q5

36 R—B7+

Escaping the threat of 36 N-K7+.

36 ...   R—Q2

Black gained a tempo having driven

White's knight from K4. Black is better because in the end he has the possibility of creating a passed king pawn while White is forced to defend.

37 RxR+   BxR

Black's freedom of movement increases with the disappearance of rooks but White's chances to block Black's advance with the knights are good too.

38 N—K1

Meeting the menace 38 N-B6.

38	...	P—K4
39	PxKP	PxP
40	K—Q2	B—B4

Taking the square K5 under control and keeping White's QB pawn under pressure.

41 N—Q1!

Aiming at the blockading square K3.

41 ... K—Q3

The sealed move. It could be expected that Black would improve the position of his king first and then try to find the best plan at home.

| 42 | N—K3 | B—K3 |
| 43 | K—Q3 | B—B2 |

Being ready for 44 K-K4?? B-N3+.

| 44 | K—B3 | K—B3 |
| 45 | K—Q3 | |

White must wait but the other side doesn't prove that there is much to be done.

45 ... K—B4

Inviting the opponent to come to K4 and eventually play for the exchange of knights.

46 K—K4

Fischer never resists such temptations to be active.

46 ... K—Q3

46 ... N-B3 would be followed by 47 N-Q3+.

47 K—Q3

47 N-B5+ NxN 48 KxN K-Q4 would be dangerous for White because the white king would be away from the true centre. Now the identical position occurs as existed after 43 moves but with Black — not White — on the move. Has it any significance here?

47	...	B—N3+
48	K—B3	K—B4
49	N—Q3+	K—Q3

49 ... BxN 50 KxB N-B6 51 K-K4 would not be dangerous for White.

50 N—K1   K—B3

50 ... N-B6 51 NxN PxN 52 K-Q2 and with 53 P-B3 there would be no square where his opponent could approach.

51 K—Q2

Waiting again.

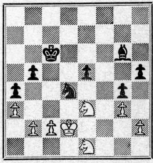

51 ... K—B4?

The only remaining chance was 51 ... P-K5! and 52 ... N-B6 and White still has problems.

52	N—Q3+	K—Q3
53	N—K1	N—K3
54	K—B3	N—Q5

Under the wrong impression that he could claim a draw by the third repetition of position, Fischer invited the referee to examine the position. Spassky, tired of vain efforts and manoeuvres, signed the score sheet before the referee could investigate the correctness of White's claim.

Draw! Fischer's lead intact for the seventh time 11½:8½!

21

Chess has entered high political circles. U.S. President's adviser Henry Kissinger announced in public that he had called Bobby Fischer in the middle of July during the crisis before the third game, when it was not known whether the match would be continued or not. Kissinger said that President Nixon did not suggest that call, but was delighted when he was told of it.

Dr. Max Euwe, President of the world chess federation, said in Reykjavik that he believed that Fischer favoured giving Spassky a rematch within a year if he took the Russian's title. Dr. Euwe said that he would support the idea.

Fischer said that he would like to defend the crown often, maybe every year instead of every three years under the F.I.D.E.'s present cycle of elimination contests. (Fischer about Soviet champions: "They take the title and then hide themselves for three years.") But, Fischer's aides denied — at this moment — that he has expressed any views on playing Spassky again.

His entourage pictured Fischer as impatient after seven consecutive draws, the longest series not only in his impressive career, but in all postwar world championship matches, the previous record being six draws in a row in Botvinnik-Petrosian in 1963 and in Petrosian-Spassky in 1966.

But, how then about Spassky, who was trailing by three points and who had only two wins over the board, both with White? He had the same pieces in the twenty-first game and could allow only one draw to his rival in the remaining four games, if the match was going to last that long. No one expected it to, including Henry Kissinger, who was pleased to give his statement before the match was ended.

As a matter of fact, Bobby could not mind draws as much as Boris, who saw his title melting, and Fischer was in a state of certain euphoria sensing the closeness of victory and had no time to think of newly appeared deficiencies in his repertoire. He just resisted the pressure, approaching his life goal, little by little. It looked to be Fischer's destiny now, for he even missed wins in the 15th and 18th games, when Spassky was impatient and was overreaching himself.

But, in the twenty-first game, Fischer — after some short period of relative creative failure — again disclosed an original idea of a deep thinker. By his magic wand he transformed the Sicilian Defence into an endgame of the Scotch Opening! Spassky could not believe his eyes when he realized what trap he had fallen into, applying an opening he never intended, even in a dream. He could not hide the disgust on his face because of the drawish position he could not avoid any more. He tried a sacrifice of the exchange, but he had to fight for a draw then. It would not have been that tragic for him, perhaps, if he had not committed suicide in the thirtieth move, allowing his opponent to make a passed pawn, which was to decide the game. They then formally adjourned until the next day.

The match was over! Robert Fischer was the first American to win the highest title in the history of chess. The match itself opened a new era in the world of chess. What next?

White: Spassky
Black: Fischer
Sicilian Defence
  1 P—K4   P—QB4
The Sicilian was a surprise even from Fischer at the final stage of the match.
  2 N—KB3   P—K3
Once again Fischer varies. Previously he played 2 ... P-Q3.
  3 P—Q4   PxP
  4 NxP   P—QR3
This version of the Paulsen line was played by Petrosian against Fischer in the seventh game of their Buenos Aires match when the Soviet grandmaster was crushed.
  5 N—QB3
Against Petrosian, Fischer played the more flexible 5 B-Q3 and after 5 ... N-QB3 6 NxN NPxN 7 0-0 P-Q4 8 P-QB4 N-B3 9 BPxP BPxP 10 PxP PxP 11 N-B3 B-K2 12 Q-R4+! outplayed his opponent. But Spassky has a different taste and Fischer knew it.
  5 ...   N—QB3
Usual is 5 ... Q-B2 but Fischer prefers to deviate from recent tournament praxis. The specific order of moves in this game is a favourite of Taimanov's.
  6 B—K3
Weak is 6 NxN NPxN 7 B-Q3 P-Q4 giving Black a strong centre. Janosevic-Tringov, Skopje 1970.
More frequently played has been 6 P-KN3 K N-K2 (6 ... P-Q3 7 B-N2 B-Q2 transposes into the Scheveningen line. Formanek-Kavalek, USA 1971) 7 N(4)-K2 (or 7 N-N3 N-R4 8 Q-R5 NxN 9 RPxN N-B3 10 B-KN5 B-K2 11 BxB QxB 12 B-N2 0-0. Timman-Radev, Tbilisi 1971) 7 ... N-N3 8 B-N2 B-B4 9 0-0 P-N4 10 N-B4 B-N2 with good counterplay. Kapengut-Taimanov, Leningrad 1971.
Interesting is 6 B-KB4 P-Q3 7 B-N3 P-K4 8 N-N3 N-B3 9 B-QB4 B-K2 10 0-0-0 0-0 11 P-QR4 P-QN3 12 Q-K2 B-N2 13 KR-Q1 Q-B2 14 B-R4 N-QN5 15 BxN BxB 16 N-Q5 with a lasting positional advantage. Janosevic-Hartoch, Amsterdam 1971.

  6 ...   N—B3
Black refrains from wasting a tempo on the customary Q-B2, and thus is ready for some action in the centre.
  7 B—Q3   P—Q4!
This is quite unexpected, designed to neutralize Spassky's favourite attacking set-up (with 8 P-B4) for White in the Paulsen line.

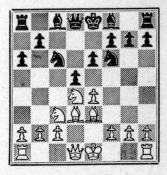

  8 PxP   PxP!
One more surprise. More cautious looks 8 ... NxP avoiding the isolated pawn in the centre, but after 9 N(4)xN (9 N(3)xN QxN is easy for Black) 9 ... PxN (9 ... NxB? 10 NxQ NxQ 11 RxN KxN 12 BxRP+) 10 B-Q4 White would be better off. This new Black set-up must have been analyzed by Fischer beforehand.
  9 0—0   B—Q3
There is a threat 10 ... N-KN5. The white KB is not best placed against Black's isolated pawn which gives free play to the black pieces and limits the activity of the white QN.
  10 NxN
White did not see any other way to activate the pair of bishops but this strengthens the Black pawn centre.
  10 ...   PxN
  11 B—Q4   0—0
Naturally not 11 ... P-B4? 12 BxN and Black's QP would be hanging.
  12 Q—B3

The same strategy as in a similar position arising from the Scotch game (see note to move 15) but it does not offer more than an even endgame.

12 ...   B—K3

Defending the QP better. Premature would be 12 ... N-N5 13 P-KR3 N-R7? (or 13 ... Q-R5 14 KR-K1) 14 Q-R5 P-N3 15 Q-R6 gaining a tempo with a mating threat. Not 12 ... B-KN5?? 13 BxN.

13   KR—K1

White took a long time for this move as he did not like a rather drawish endgame, yet he has no better choice.

13   ...   P—B4
14   BxN   QxB
15   QxQ   PxQ

This position shows White's idea, but Black has no problems for this is almost identical to a position arising from the Scotch game after 1 P-K4 P-K4 2 N-KB3 N-QB3 3 N-B3 N-B3 4 P-Q4 PxP 5 NxP B-N5 6 NxN NPxN 7 B-Q3 P-Q4 8 PxP PxP 9 0-0 0-0 10 B-KN5 P-B3 11 Q-B3 B-Q3 12 QR-K1 (otherwise 12 ... B-K4) P-KR3 13 BxN QxB 14 QxQ PxQ. The differences here are that Black's QRP has advanced one square and not his KRP, and White has his KR on K1 instead of his QR.

16   QR—Q1   KR—Q1

It is queer how quite a different semi-closed opening brought an almost identical position and endgame to that known from an open system such as the Scotch Game. It is certain that White had never intended to reach this position when making his first move.

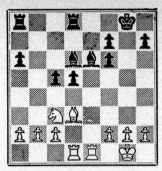

17   B—K2

Trying to build the pressure on Black's QP.

17   ...   QR—N1
18   P—QN3

The Black QP is taboo: 18 NxP? BxN 19 RxB BxP+.

18   ...   P—B5

The threat 19 ... B-QN5 makes it impossible for White to keep his pressure on Black's QP.

19   NxP?

A surprise. The sacrifice of the exchange looks correct and White hopes to get endgame chances when capturing Black's Q-side pawns. But there are hidden dangers in the position.

19   ...   BxN
20   RxB   BxP+

If first 20 ... PxP the black QR pawn would be hanging.

21   KxB   RxR
22   BxP   R—Q7!

Attack is the best form of defence!

23   BxRP   RxQBP

Black has to lessen the number of passed pawns on the queen side.

24   R—K2

Otherwise the material advantage would be clearly on Black's side.

24   ...   RxR

The best. The other rook will come onto the seventh rank.

25   BxR   R—Q1
26   P—R4

The best chance.

26   ...   R—Q7
27   B—B4   R—R7

Not 27 ... RxP? 28 P-R5 R-R7 29 P-R6 K-B1 30 P-QN4 R-R5 31 P-N5 RxB 32 P-R7 R-QR5 33 P-N6 and White wins.

28   K—N3   K—B1
29   K—B3   K—K2

30   P—KN4?

A terrible mistake. 30 P-N3 was safer.

30   ...   P—B4
31   PxP   P—B3

Black has a passed pawn now and that is the most that he could hope for with those doubled pawns.

32   B—N8

Better was 32 K-N4.

32   ...   P—R3
33   K—N3   K—Q3
34   K—B3   R—R8
35   K—N2

The threat was 35 ... R-KN8 to cut the white king off from the black passed pawn.

35   ...   K—K4
36   B—K6   K—B5
37   B—Q7

White has problems avoiding zugzwang.

37   ...   R—QN8!

Black is playing for a win.

38   B—K6   R—N7

On 38 ... K-N5 White would have a reply in 39 B-N8 when Black cannot take the pawn because of 40 B-R7+. With the move in the game Black moves the rook from an exposed square.

39   B—B4   R—R7

Again not 39 ... KxP because of 40 P-R5 R-R7 41 P-R6 as mentioned in the note to move 27.

40   B—K6   P—R4

Adjourned..White sealed.

Black's 40th move was not the most precise. He should have played 40 ... K-N5! first and then 41 ... P-R4 taking control of all the squares in front of the white king. If White did not seal 41 K-R3 then Black's wrong order of moves would not matter e.g. 41 K-R3 K-N4 (41 ... RxBP is wrong because of 42 P-R5 R-QR7 43 P-R6 RxRP — the threat was 44 B-B4 and P-N4 — 44 K-R4 with a draw) 42 P-B3 K-B5 43 B-B7 KxP(B4) 44 BxP K-B5 45 B-K8 R-QN7 and Black wins, but 43 B-Q5 KxP 44 K-N3 was a chance to fight on.

41   B—Q7?

The sealed move made after a short reflection. Probably Spassky momentarily lost his drive. Now 41 ... K-N5 puts things right again for Black: 42 B-B6 (otherwise comes P-R5-R6 with a mating attack) 42 ... P-R5 43 B-B3+ KxP 44 B-B6 K-N5 45 B-B3+ (a must) K-B5 46 B-B6 R-B7 and 47 ... R-B6 preventing White from controlling the white squares, decides the issue.

White resigns! The final score 12½:8½ in favour of Robert Fischer — the new chess champion of the world!

IN RETROSPECT

Among the world champions since the war, Boris Spassky has distinguished himself. During a relatively short period of five years he came victorious out of personal duels with a most exquisite group of contemporary grandmasters - Keres, Geller, Tal, Larsen, Korchnoi and Petrosian. No other world champion could boast such an impressive list of triumphs in matches.

At the same time, Robert Fischer was growing alongside him into another chess giant who, with his general results and high percentages, outclassed the achievements not only of his contemporaries, but of any individual in the whole history of world chess.

Years had to go by, and many difficulties had to be overcome, until the match between these two players in their prime became reality, the match which every chess enthusiast considered as the most wishful chess event of our century. By happy coincidence - after a quarter of a century of supremacy by one country - it was also the first clash at the top in the spirit of healthy sporting rivalry between the best representatives of two different parts of the world.

All that gives a clue to the unexpected chess fever which overwhelmed continents during those two months in Reykjavik. The match opened a new, unforeseen chapter in the history of this noble game, which has existed modestly for more than one thousand years, only now to be discovered by a good part of mankind as the best game ever invented by the human mind.

Yet, the peculiar attitude of the challenger almost brought about the cancellation of the match. Several miracles had to occur simultaneously - like in a tale - in order to save the competition and the interests of world chess. The president of F.I.D.E. and ex-world champion, Dr. Max Euwe, and the German grandmaster Lothar Schmid as referee, intervened with the sudden idea of two days postponement, just to buy time in a legal but irregular way. The title holder, Spassky, was generous in not disagreeing with this. The Icelandic organizers were extremely patient, and another sponsor from another country - Mr. Jim Slater - offered to double the prize fund. All that happened - without any pre-arrangement - in less than 48 hours and Robert Fischer finally appeared at the hall.

A very attractive match to a few millions of chess fans was transformed into an unbelievable sensation to hundreds of millions of non-playing readers throughout the world. By the end of the world championship in Reykjavik, many millions of them were playing readers.

The merits of Fischer and Spassky were enormous and twofold. Not taking into account a few weak moments, understandable under such a strain, it was chess of the highest professional class that was played in the match. Many systems and opening lines, recognized and applied for years in the most important international competitions by the leading grandmasters of the world, will have to be completely re-appraised after only twenty or so games played in Iceland. This match will influence the development of ideas in future tournament praxis.

Apart from the chess aspect, there was a strange psychological situation from which arose a large controversy in public opinion. Fischer's spokesman explained in one of his many letters to the referee, Schmid, the frequency of American demands by saying that it is known "how dear to the challenger's heart is the perfection of conditions for grandmaster chess". It is also true, as a 'Time' magazine reader stated, that "Fischer alone has probably brought more prize money and better playing conditions to tournament chess than all the greats combined", and another reader said that "for the first time in chess history there has come forward someone who has elevated chess to the category of a contest in which the rewards should be proportionate to the ability of the contestants".

At the same time, Fischer's tireless insistence both on big issues and petty details, created an atmosphere of confusion and tension which could easily have influenced the calm necessary to his opponent. It seems that Spassky tried to retaliate with a few protests of a similar kind when the match was close to its end. But, the puzzle remains whether Fischer's attitude was a 'mean device to destroy the fighting spirit of the champion', or just the defence of his principles and the continuation of his lifelong struggle for 'perfect conditions'.

Spassky was magnanimous and apparently confident at the beginning of the match. He felt well prepared, and he was, except for a limited area - those lines that Fischer had never played before. The challenger grasped the situation excellently and avoided everything that his opponent could expect, going from one surprise to another. As Black, he didn't play the King's Indian or Gruenfeld Defence, and as White, even refrained for a while from the king's pawn, his favourite first move all his life. Spassky was taken aback by the all-round knowledge of the American grandmaster, and after ten games was on the brink of a catastrophe.

Only then the title holder realized that the direction of his preparations was the wrong one. He had tried stubbornly to outplay the challenger in systems where Fischer had more knowledge and experience. In the second half, Spassky turned back to his best weapons from other competitions, being then ready to take his share of risks in Fischer's double-edged lines. It was now the duel of rivals on about the same highest level, but nothing could change the established large difference in points.

There were exciting moments at the very end of the match, too, but Spassky, stunned by Fischer's rapid reactions in very complicated positions (can we ascribe this speed as a superhuman quality of the new ruler in chess), here and there missed his best opportunity, as did Fischer himself. In general, Fischer gave an impression of being more at ease in finding the right moves, while Spassky spent more time on the same purpose. When Fischer was asked why he almost never allowed himself to get into time pressure, he replied: "It is not chess any more."

The new champion advocates the highest professional approach to the game and sets new standards for grandmasters, who will be obliged to give their best in international competitions. Therefore, Robert Fischer enjoys the respect of the chess world.

The American grandmaster Robert Byrne played in the very strong Alekhine Memorial Tournament in Moscow in November/December 1971. He was asked for his opinion on the result of the Fischer-Spassky match and was widely quoted in the Soviet press as follows:-

"Fischer will win by 12½ to 8½ and will be World Champion for the next twelve years!"